AN EXAMINATION

OF THE

English Ancestry

OF

GEORGE WASHINGTON,

SETTING FORTH THE EVIDENCE TO CONNECT HIM

WITH THE

WASHINGTONS OF SULGRAVE AND BRINGTON.

BY.
HENRY F WATERS, A.M.

Reprinted from the N. E. Historical and Genealogical Register for
October, 1889.

1889.

Dedicated to

JAMES J. GOODWIN OF HARTFORD, CONNECTICUT,

IN GRATEFUL RECOGNITION OF HIS FRIENDSHIP AND HIS LIBERALITY
IN SUPPORTING THESE RESEARCHES.

THE ANCESTRY OF WASHINGTON.

In the July number of the N. E. Historical and Genealogical Register I announced some discoveries about the Washington family which I then expected to publish among my Gleanings for that number. Very soon after that announcement I discovered some additional facts so interesting and important, and, apparently, so clearly pointing to the true line of ancestry of our first President that I thought it best, after consulting my friends in England and America, to withhold the matter thus promised until I could add to it these new facts and publish them together, in order that their due relations to each other might be the more apparent. I do not claim to have made an exhaustive study of the Washington Genealogy. That is not my province, as the readers of my Gleanings must, by this time, be well aware. My function rather is similar to that of the prospector who finds the hidden lode of rich ore and makes it known to the miners who may wish to follow up and develop the vein more thoroughly. It is for me to search out and discover the clews and place them in the hands of the specialists who come after, that they may be guided in the right direction and so not waste their efforts in random labor on unfruitful ground. If, in addition, I do occasionally, as in the present case, furnish evidence illustrating a pedigree more at length, it is simply because in my extended wanderings over a wide field I have naturally gathered such facts as have come to my notice and saved them for the general good.

Before entering upon the story of these discoveries let me first state the problem which was to be solved, and refer to one or two attempts which have been made at its solution in the past. The American line of ancestry had been traced back clearly to a John Washington who, with his brother Lawrence, crossed the ocean to Virginia about 1657. The problem was to find their parentage and ancestry in England. It was known that both of them made wills which were proved in Virginia. These wills, or abstracts of them, will I doubt not accompany this paper.*

---

* Nothing can be added to the statement of Bishop Meade, in regard to the wills of the two emigrants, of which documents he gives abstracts. The will of John Washington was then recorded at Westmoreland Court House, "in an old book of wills, though in a somewhat mutilated form." Since then the book has disappeared, probably during the time of the late war. The will of "John Washington, of Washington parish, in the county of Westmoreland, in Virginia, gentleman," was dated February 26, 1675, and proved January 10, 1677. He directs his body to be buried on the plantation upon which he lived, by the side of his wife and two children. He divides a number of landed estates between his second and surviving wife and his children, John, Lawrence and Anne, and also his proper-

Sir Isaac Heard, then Garter King of Arms, began in 1791 the discussion of this problem, as I learn from an essay on this subject written by the late Col. Joseph L. Chester, LL.D., D.C.L., and published in the "Herald and Genealogist" (London), September, 1866, and republished in America in "The Heraldic Journal" (Boston), October, 1866, and again in "The N. E. Historical and Genealogical Register" (Boston), January, 1867. From this paper I quote the following extract:

Sir Isaac took as the basis of his pedigree the Heraldic Visitations of Northamptonshire, in which the Washington family was included. Starting with the well-known fact that the first emigrants of the name to Virginia were two brothers named John and Lawrence Washington, who left England for that colony about the year 1657, he found recorded in the Visitation of 1618 the names of John and Lawrence described as sons of Lawrence Washington of Sulgrave in that county, who had died in the year 1616. The names being identical with those of the Virginia emigrants, and the period at which they lived not altogether inappropriate, Sir Isaac *assumed* their personal identity; and on this assumption constructed his pedigree, deducing the descent of the American President through this heraldic family of Northamptonshire from the still more ancient one of the name in Lancashire. It is but just to the memory of Sir Isaac to say that he himself only regarded the pedigree as a conjectural one, and that he took the precaution to leave on the margin of his own copy a note (which was seen and copied by Mr. Sparks) to the effect that he was not clearly satisfied that the connection of the President with the Sulgrave family was or could be substantiated."

Mr. Baker, in his History of Northamptonshire, followed Sir Isaac's example, but without any reservation. He confidently asserted that John, son of Lawrence Washington of Sulgrave, was of South Cave, co. York, and emigrated to America (from whom, in the third generation, President Washington was derived), and that Lawrence (the brother of this John) was a student at Oxford, 1622, and emigrated to America with his brother.

The above pedigree was accepted by all as authoritative until 1863, when Isaac J. Greenwood, Esq., of New York, threw

ty in England. He leaves £1000 to his brother-in-law, Thomas Pope; and £1000 and four thousand weight of tobacco to his sister, who had come or was coming over to this country. He makes his wife and brother Lawrence his executors.

The will of Lawrence Washington, of Rappahannock county, dated September 27, 1675, proved January 6, 1677, is presumed to be still on record. Bishop Meade's abstract agrees with the complete copy printed in Welles's book, which latter document is attested by James Roy Micou, Clerk of Essex County, Va. It gives all his property in England to his daughter Mary and the heirs of her body; failing them to children John and Ann. He then mentions his loving wife Jane and her two children, John and Ann, both under age, and the land which came to him in the right of his wife, on the south side of the river, formerly belonging to Capt. Alexander Flemming. Gives two hundred acres of land to Alexander Barrow. Appoints wife Jane, executrix, brother Col. John Washington and friend Thomas Hawkins, overseers.

We now know that John Washington was born prior to 1634, and Lawrence was born in 1635. Hence they were aged respectively about 24 and 22 years in 1657, when they are said to have emigrated to Virginia. Nothing in the wills is decisive of the point whether either or both married prior to their leaving England, but it is more probable than not, and our English friends should be on the look-out for such marriages. In Virginia there may yet be found some dates of grants or purchases of land which will aid in showing their progress there.—WILLIAM H. WHITMORE.

doubts upon it in a paper communicated to the N. E. Historical and Genealogical Register for July of that year, by suggesting that John and Lawrence, the sons of Lawrence Washington of Sulgrave, were too old to have been the emigrants to Virginia. He also suggested that the Virginians might have been descended from Sir William Washington of Packington, Kn^t., eldest son of Lawrence of Sulgrave.

In Col. Chester's Essay, already referred to, the theory advanced by Sir Isaac Heard and so confidently asserted by Baker in his History, was thoroughly disproved by the array of evidence brought forward which showed that John, the son of Lawrence Washington of Sulgrave, was clearly Sir John Washington of Thrapston, both of whose wives died in England, the latter (Dame Dorothy) outliving her husband; while it is well known that John Washington, the emigrant, buried his first wife (whose name is unknown) in Virginia, and married, secondly, Ann (Pope) whom he appointed executrix of his will, jointly with his brother Lawrence. The children of Sir John, of Thrapston, were Mordaunt, John and Philip. The children of John, of Virginia, were John, Lawrence and Anne. Col. Chester also showed how improbable it was that Lawrence, the brother of Sir John, could have been the Lawrence who emigrated to Virginia, by proving that he was a clergyman of the established church; while Lawrence, of Virginia, simply styled himself "gentleman," a most unlikely thing for him to do, if he were in holy orders.

Col. Chester contented himself with thus completely demolishing the former theory, without setting up a new one in its place: so the original problem was left unchanged. On the American side of the water we had a complete chain running back from the President to the first settler of the name. There the chain, like the vast majority of American pedigrees, was broken short off, at the water's edge. The task which lay before me, on my arrival in England in 1883, was to drag the depths in all directions, with the hope of picking up, somewhere, the lost end of the English line to which the American line belonged. Fortunately I did not come over to hunt for Washingtons alone: such a task would have seemed well nigh appalling. I was on the lookout for references to every American family of English origin, whatever the name; and the tedium and monotony of my toilsome search has been relieved by almost daily discoveries, some of exceptional value and importance, like those relating to the Harvard family, the famous Rogers family of New England, the family of Roger Williams, and others of less interest, perhaps, to the general reader, but full of interest, doubtless, to those engaged in the investigation of the genealogies of the special families mentioned in my notes.

At first I gleaned over the whole field for Washingtons and found them in various counties, (e.g.) Yorkshire, Westmoreland, Lancashire, Leicestershire, Worcestershire, Warwickshire, Northamptonshire, Oxfordshire, Buckinghamshire, Berkshire, Hertfordshire, Middlesex, Kent, Surrey, Wiltshire, Devonshire, Essex, Suffolk and Norfolk. In the fall of 1884 or the spring of 1885 I made a very important discovery which led me to limit my field of search, by finding a point on the soil of the mother country to which I could make fast the end of the American line. It appears that upon the death of Lawrence Washington of Virginia, although his will, as I have said, was proved in Virginia, letters of administration on his goods, &c., were granted in England, as follows:—

"Mense Maij 1677 tricesimo die Em^t Com^o Edmundo Jones principali creditori Laurentii Washington nuper de Luton in Comitatu Bedford sed apud Virginiã in partibus transmarinis decedeñ ad adstrand bona jura et credita dict deft de bene etc jurat."   Admon. Act Book (P. C. C.)

This was a great step, and it behoved me to make a careful search all around Luton and its immediate neighborhood for further traces. This parish is in the extreme southern part of Bedfordshire, on a kind of tongue or neck jutting into the neighboring county of Herts. For more than four years I have borne this discovery in mind, and in all that time have never let a will made by any one in that part of Bedfordshire or of Hertfordshire pass under my notice without the most careful scrutiny; and I made known my discovery to most of my English friends, that they might keep their eyes open in that quarter. I had already, to be sure, found an Adam Washington, gentleman, seated at Brent Pelham, Herts, whose father, Adam Washington, citizen and mercer of London, was evidently of the Washington family of Grayrigg in Kendal, Westmoreland, but I had examined the wills relating to them without getting any light about the emigrants to Virginia.

Good fortune, which has so often befriended me in my genealogical work, once more rewarded my plodding toil with bountiful generosity; and this time she added to the value of her gift by bestowing it through the hand of a friend. It happened in this way. While the official work of indexing certain bonds, once belonging to the Hitchin Registry of the Archdeaconry of Huntingdon, was recently in progress in the Probate Registry, one came to light of which the following is an abstract:

A Bond of John Dagnall, of Grove in the parish of Tring, in co. Herts, Yeoman, and William Roades of Middle Claydon, in co. Bucks., Gen., in the sum of one thousand pounds, dated 29 January 1649 (50), for the administration of the goods &c. of Andrew Knowling, of Tring in the county of Herts., gen., lately deceased, with the will annexed, during the minority of Lawrence Washington the younger, at that time of the age of fourteen years; also for their faithful conduct as guardians or curators of the said Lawrence Washington &c.

Tring is but twelve miles, or a little more, from Luton,* and the

---

* See map front of title page. Tring is described in the Gazetteer as a parish and market town in Hertfordshire, 28 miles west of Hertford. Acres 7390, houses 667, population 3488

two towns are connected, by way of Dunstable and, thence, along the old Icknield Way which runs from Dunstable to the immediate neighborhood of Tring. It was altogether probable then that here was the early home of Lawrence Washington of Luton and Virginia. As I was absent from London at the time of this discovery, my friend took the pains to hunt up the will of Mr. Knowling in order that he might make an abstract of it so as to gratify me with the sight of it upon my next visit at Somerset House. Since then, however, I have made a full copy of this will, which is here given:—

In the Name of God Amen the Thirteenth day of January in the yeare of o^r Lord god one Thousand Sixe hundred fforty and Nine I Andrew Knowling of Tring in the County of Hertf' gent' being weake of body but of sound and pfect memory (thanks be giuen to Allmighty God) doe make & ordaine this to be my last will & testam^t in mann^r & forme following vizt Inprimis I bequeath my soulle into the handes of allmighty God my most mercifull Creato^r assuredly trusting through the merrittes death & passion of my Lord & only Savio^r Jesus Christ to enioye eternall life & my body to thearth from whence it came to be decently buried. Item I give to the poore of the Towne of Tring and the upp Hamblettes the some of Twentie Shillings to be paid within one month next after my decease. Item I give to the poore of Willsterne within the said pish of Tring the some of Twenty Shillings to be paid in sorte and mann^r as aforesaid. Item I give to the poore of Wigginton in the said County of Herts Tenn Shillings to be paid as aforesaid: Item I will give and bequeath unto Lawrance Washington the younger (my godsonne) All my freehould Landes and Tenem^{ts} whatsoeu^r lying and being within the pish of Tring aforesaid or else where within the Realme of England. To haue and to hould the same to him and his heires for euer. Item I give and bequeath unto Amphilis Washington my daughter in lawe (& mother of the said Lawrance) the some of Threescore poundes of Curr^t mony of England to be paid her within six months after my decease. Item I give and bequeath unto Elizabeth ffitzherbert one other of my daughters in Lawe the some of ffortye pounds of Curr^t mony to be paid in sorte and mann^r as is last above mencōned. Item I give and bequeath unto William Roades my sonne in Lawe the some of Tenn poundes of Curr^t mony to be paid within sixe months next after my decease: Item I give and bequeath unto the said Elizabeth ffitzherbert all my corne & graine whatsoeu^r now within doores or without. Item I give and bequeath unto the Two daughters of my late daughter in Lawe Susann Billing deceased begotten of her body by her late husband John Billing of Lillington in the County of Buck, Tallowe Chauudler, Tenn poundes apeece to be paid within sixe monthes after my decease And my will is that if either of the said Two children dye before her Legacie shalbecome due

in 1831. It is perhaps best known by the popular, though unfounded rhyme, applied to one of the ancestors of John Hampden, who was said to have forfeited three manors for striking the Black Prince with his racket when they quarrelled at tennis.

"Tring, Wing and Ivanhoe,
For striking of a blow,
Hampden did forego,
And glad he could escape so."

Unfortunately neither of these manors ever belonged to a Hampden. (See Notes and Queries, 3rd S., v. p. 176.)

Luton is a town in Bedfordshire, with 15,500 acres and about 6000 population. A glance at the map shows however that Tring and Luton are but a few miles apart and a resident in one town might easily be well known in the other.—WILLIAM H. WHITMORE.

and payable Then I will that the Legacie of her dying shalbe paid to the other surviving. Item I give and bequeath unto John Washington, William Washington, Elizabeth Washington, Margarett Washington & Martha Washington (children of the said Amphilis Washington my daughter in Lawe) The some of Eight and Twenty poundes a peece of Curr^t mony to be paid to them att theire seu'all & respective Ages of One and Twenty years, To be putt out in the meane tyme for theire best benefitt & advantage And my will and meaning is that if any of the said ffiue children vizt John, William, Elizabeth, Margarett and Martha Washington shall happen to die before his her or theire Legacie or Legacies shall become due & payable, That then the Legacie or Legacies of him, her or them soe dying shalbe equally divided amongst the rest of them the said five children surviving. Item I give and bequeath unto Susan Emmerton of Tring aforesaid widd the some of ffifty shillings to be paid to her within sixe monthes after my decease. All the rest of my goodes Cattles and chattles & prsonall estate not heerin given and disposed of, my debts and Legacies heerin giuen paid and my fun^{r}all chardges defrayed I give unto the said Lawrance Washington the young^r my Godsonne whome I make sole and wholle executo^r of this my last Will and Testam^t And I earnestly desire John Dagnall of Groue within the pish of Tring aforesaid yeoman John Lake of Willst^{r}ne aforesaid Gent' & the said Willm Roades and Elizabeth ffitzherbert to take upon them (for the sole benefitt & behoofe of the said Lawrance Washing' myne Executo^r) The admi'stracon of my goodes & Chattles during the minoritie of the said Lawrance Washing' & to see the due pformance of this my said Will, And I doe giue unto them Tenn shillinges a peece All former Wills by me made I doe heerby Revoake & repeale and declare this to be my last Will and Testament. In Wittnes Whereof I the said Andrew Knowling haue heereunto putt my hand and seale the day and yeare first above written.

                                          ANDREW KNOWLING.

Sealed subscribed published and   *A* his m^{r}ke
  deliu'ed in the p'nce of
    John ffitzherbert   William Dagnalle
    Thomas Norman   James Benning, his m^{r}ke
                                I B

Itm I will this to be pt of my Will vizt I giue and bequeath unto Wm Knowling beau^r maker in old Bridewell Lond' the some of fower pounds to buy him a Ring

                                William Dagnalle
                                James [I B] Benning his m^{r}ke
                                Thomas Norman
                                John ffitzherbert (testibus)

Vicesimo nono die Mensis Januarij Anno dñi stilo Anglie 1649 apud Whethampsted p m^{r}m Gulielmū Dauis in Artibus Magr̄m surrogatū Veñrlis viri Johañis Jackson in legibus bacchalaurei Offiĩs etc. Cofñissa fuit Adm̃stracõ oiū et singlorū bonorū iuriū etc hmõi Andree Knowlinge gen'osi nup de Tryng defuncti unacū testañto suo hmõi annexo Johanni Dagnall et Guilielmo Roades in testfñio prd̄co nominatis quos dñs constituit in Curatores seu Gardianos Laurentio Washington Juniori dc̄i testañti executori etatis 14 aōrū vel circiter ac quibus acceptañ officiū in se Gardianorū seu Curatorū p^{r}d de bene et fidelr̄ adm'strañd etc. Obligtur dc̄i Johēs Dagnall de Tryng p^{r}d Yeoman et Guilfñus Roades de Middle Claydon Cofñ Bucks: geñ in 1000^{li}

Through this happy discovery we are at last introduced, in all probability, to the immediate family of the two emigrants to Virginia, their mother, brother, three sisters, uncle, aunts, cousins and grandfather by marriage; for I suppose we may reasonably infer the marriage of Mr. Andrew Knowling with the widowed mother of William Roades, Amphillis Washington, Elizabeth Fitzherbert and Susanna Billing. The name of the husband of Amphillis is not given, but from the fact that the executor and residuary legatee named in the will is called Lawrence Washington the younger, we may also conjecture that his father's name was Lawrence.

A visit to Tring came next in order. There I was most cordially received by the Vicar of that parish, the Rev. W. Quennell, who, having a taste for such investigations and being evidently pleased that I had traced the Washington family to his parish, was kind enough to assist me. The Registers previous to 1634, I found, were not in very good order, and I made a rather hasty examination of them. That beginning 1634 was entitled "A Regester Booke conteaning all the names hereafter Named either Baptized, Married or Buried. Bought by Maister Andreu Knolinge, Richard Hunton" (and others, whose names are given and who are called churchwardens). In it I found the following :—

Baptisms.

Crisames senc our Ladie daye Anno Dom̄ 1635 Layaranc sonn of Layarance Washington June the xxiii^d

Baptized senc our Ladye daye Anno dom 1636 Elizabeth da of Mr Larranc Washington Aug xvii

Baptized senc Mickellmas daye Anno Dom̄ 1641 William sonn of Mr Larrance Washenton baptized the xiiijth daij

Burials.

Andrew Knolling was bur^d this xxith of January 1649.
Edward Fitzherbert bur. the iii of May 1654.
Mrs Washington bur: ye xix of Jan: 1654.
Mr John Dagnall of the Grove bur^d 17 Aug. 1691.

This confirmed my conjecture that the father's name was Lawrence; and, from the fact that the son was called "Lawrence Washington the younger" in Mr. Knowling's will, it is plain that the father was alive when that will was made, in January, 1649–50. I did not find the baptisms of John, Margaret or Martha Washington, and could not therefore determine the age of John Washington at the date of his immigration to Virginia. Fortunately this was settled, near enough, in another way. My next discovery was the following :—

February 1655 The Eighth day Lres of adc̄on yssued forth to John Washington the nr̄all and lawfull sone of Amphillis Washington late of Tring in the County of Hertford deĉd to adr̄ter the goodes Chēlls and debtes of the said deĉd Hee beeing first sworne truly to adr̄ter &c.

Admon. Act Book (P. C. C.), 42.

From this I drew two inferences: first, that Mr. Lawrence Washington, husband of Amphillis and father of John and Lawrence, had predeceased his wife; and, secondly, that John Washington, to whom the letters of Admon. issued, was the eldest son. As we have seen, Lawrence was baptized in the summer of 1635 and Elizabeth in 1636. John could not have been born later than 1634, and must have been at least twenty-one years of age at the grant of admon., and twenty-three in 1657, the date of emigration.

My next endeavor was to find, if possible, the wills of William Roades, Elizabeth Fitzherbert and John Dagnall. The first, which I soon found, was as follows:—

William Roades (residence not mentioned) 19 September 1657, proved 17 November 1658. To my son John twelve pence and to his wife and two children, William and Anne Roades, twelve pence apiece. To my grand child William Lee twelve pence, and my best bible after my wife's decease. The residue to be divided into four parts, of which one part to my wife and the other three parts to my daughters Hannah, Hester and Sarah Roades. My wife to be executrix.

The will was proved by Hannah Roades, the widow.
Wootton (P. C. C.), 608.

As his place of abode had not been mentioned I called for the Probate Act Book for that year, and found that the testator was of Middle Claydon, Bucks.

The will of Mr. John Dagnall, of Grove, I also found after something of a search, but got no help from it. He only named his immediate family. My search after Mrs. Fitzherbert was a much longer one. At last I came upon the wills of a family of that name, settled in Oxfordshire, which seemed to me worth saving.

Robert Fitzherbert of Begbrooke, Oxon. Esq., 2 August 1636, proved 22 November 1636. Mentions children of brother William Fitzherbert, sister Dyonis Fitzherbert, children of sister Morgan (William, James and Mary), John Fitzherbert, one of the sons of brother Humfrey Fitzherbert deceased, niece Anne Clement, brother Edward Fitzherbert and his children, John, Edward and Mary, sister Ursula and her children, Thomas, Solymie and Mary, and her grandchild Robert Kente. Thomas Leeke (alias Leake) son of my half brother John Leake deceased. Pile (P. C. C.), 107.

Edward Fitzharbert of Middleston Stony, Oxon. Gen^t, 10 June 1639. My body to be buried in the parish Church of Middleston Stony, near son Nicholas, deceased. To wife Elizabeth my lease of house and two yards &c. in same parish. Eldest son John, son Edward and daughter Mary Fitzherbert. Brother John Fitzharbert of Bagbrooke Esq. to be executor.

The executor having renounced commission issued to Elizabeth Fitzharbert, the widow, 5 May, 1642. Cambell (P. C. C.), 70.

John Fitzherbert the elder, of Begbrooke, Oxon. Esq., 1 April 1649, proved 25 April 1649. Mentions nephew John, son of brother Edward deceased (evidently regarded as heir), nephew Edward and niece Mary Fitzherbert, also children of deceased brother Edward; kinsman Mr. Thomas Hinton and Mr. John Garrett, both of Great Tue, Oxon. The witnesses were John Fitzherbert, Elizabeth Fitzherbert and John Goad, cleric. Fairfax (P. C. C.), 49.

John Fitzherbert, of Bedbrooke, Oxon. Esq., 26 May 1658, proved 23 March 1660. Mentions friends Thomas Hinton of Banbury, Oxon., and John Garrett, of Great Tewe, Oxon., Gen^t; my manor of Begbrooke; wife Anne; my three younger sons, William, Thomas and John (under fourteen); eldest son Francis; daughters Elizabeth and Mary Fitzherbert; father in law Edward Atkins, one of the Justices of the Common Bench.
May (P. C. C.), 44.

My reason for saving these wills was that I guessed Mrs. Elizabeth Fitzherbert might be the widow of Edward Fitzherbert. Her son John was a witness of Mr. Knowling's will. Her son Edward was buried at Tring. (It was her nephew John, however, who inherited the manor of Begbrooke.) This was for a long time only a guess, until, at last, it was converted into a certainty by the following will:

Elizabeth Fitzherbert, of Much Waltham, Essex, widow, 23 February, 1684, proved 29 November 1689. She devised all her lands and tenements &c. in Tring, Herts., and the houses and lands called Makins, in Middleton Stony, Oxford, and all her estate and rights &c. in them to John Freeman, of Luton, Bedfordshire, gentleman, and Samuel Marshall of Norstend, Much Waltham, Esq. (in trust) during the joint lives of John Rotheram, of Much Waltham, Esq., and Mary his wife, her daughter, to pay the rents, issues and profits of the said houses in Tring &c. to the said Mary, with other provisions in case of their deaths; and the said John Freeman, of Luton, was to be executor of the will. Ent (P. C. C.), 154.

Although somewhat disappointed that neither of these wills mentioned the Washingtons and so I was not yet possessed of the positive evidence for which I had been seeking in order to prove beyond a doubt the identity of the Virginians with John and Lawrence of Tring, yet I was, on the whole, satisfied with that of Mrs. Fitzherbert, which, by its mention of Luton, strengthened the probabilities of the case. And I was well aware that the family of Rotheram was a very important one in Luton and its neighborhood (see the Visitations of Bedfordshire), and that through marriages they were connected with Tring as well.

A pedigree of this family of Fitzherbert may be found in the Visitations of Oxford (Harleian So. Pub.).

All this time I was seeking to find an answer to the question, who was this Mr. Lawrence Washington, the father of these children? That he was styled "Mr." on the church Register meant that he was either a clergyman or a person of some importance, and I had a suspicion, which I hardly dared to breathe, that he might be that parson of Purleigh, about whom I have for years had the feeling that if he could only be hunted down we might possibly be able to dispel the mystery enveloping the lineage of Washington. It is perhaps needless to say that I determined to watch most carefully for even the slightest indication of a clew which might lead to the identification of this Lawrence Washington of Tring. First of all, it seemed best to examine with the greatest care all the papers connected with the probate of Mr. Knowling's will, partly for the purpose of making the full copy of that will which I intended to publish *in extenso*, and partly in the hope that I might come upon something or other, not yet known, which would help me a stage further in my research. I found the will, as I have already given it. I found also an inventory of the personal property of the testator, appraised 23 January, 1649, at 534£. 11ˢ. 8ᵈ.

Connected with these papers was a bond of guardianship made by John Dagnall of Grove in the parish of Tring, co. Herts, Yeoman, in the sum of fifty pounds, dated 29 January, 1649 (50), as guardian and curator of the two daughters of Susan Billing deceased, begotten of her body by her late husband John Billing, of Lillington in the co. of Bucks, tallow chandler, the said John Dagnall having been appointed their guardian, &c., for the reason that he was the husband of Elizabeth Dagnall, sister* by the mother to the said two daughters.

It will be noticed that this bond was made on the very same day that the will of Mr. Knowling was produced and Admon. granted, in court at Whethampsted, and the bond was undoubtedly drawn up and signed there.

I then saw a little bit of paper, doubled or folded upon itself, which upon opening seemed about three inches long and from an inch and a half to two inches wide, and covered with writing. Seeing, at a glance, that it was evidently an official memorandum of the issuing of the letters of guardianship and of the oath taken by Mr. Dagnall for the faithful performance of his trust, I did not read it through but at once set about copying it in full, little realizing the start of surprise and gratification I should experience when I should come to the end of what proved to be the most valuable and important bit of genealogical evidence that I ever saw or ever expect to see in the course of my gleanings. This little memorandum was as follows:—

Mᵈᵘ qd 29° die Januarij Anno dñi 1649° apud Whethamsted concessæ fuerunt lr̃æ Curatoriæ ad lites dnabus filiabus Susannæ Benning defi legatariis in testm̃o hum̃oi Andreæ Knowlinge p̃recup-acõne legatorũ eisdem in dc̃o testm̃o donat̃ et de disposicõne eorundẽ ad usũ et commodũ dc̃arũ filiarũ duran earũ respẽ minori aetate et fidelr̃ se gerend̃ etc. et de redd̃o Compt̃o etc Johñi Dagnall de Grove pochiæ de Tring marito Elizabethæ materterræ dc̃arũ filiarũ iurat̃ eto corã

pñte me Guil: Rolfe   Laurentio Washington
nõrio pubc̃o   in Art: magro Surrog̃: Om̃lis
                etc hac vice

Oblig̃tur dc̃us Johẽs Dagnall in 50ᴴ.

It will be noted that Susanna's name in this memorandum is Benning, instead of Billing, a confusion of the two liquid sounds l

---

* In the original "Aunte" had been first written, and then a line drawn through it and "sister" written above, with a caret beneath the line.—H. F. W.

and n which may be noticed in other languages as well as English. Moreover "*materteræ*" (aunt by the mother) is left uncorrected. The correction, however, was made in the bond, which is in the English language. Probably Mr. Dagnall read it over before signing and noticed the error.

Here we have proof of identification, and of the most positive and conclusive character. There cannot be the least doubt that this Lawrence Washington, M.A., was the husband of Amphillis and the father of her children. He was there in the Archdeacon's Court at Whethampsted, evidently to protect the interests of that wife and those children, who, under the will presented and allowed in court that day, were to receive the bulk of Mr. Knowling's personal estate, while the second son, Lawrence, as the acknowledged heir of his godfather and the executor of his will, was to inherit the real estate of the deceased and all the residuum of the personal estate after the debts, legacies and funeral expenses and other charges should have been settled and paid. There can be but little doubt that this same Lawrence Washington, M.A., who was acting as temporary Surrogate in the Archdeacon's Court on this occasion, was a clergyman; for that court was an ecclesiastical one, and the office of Surrogate in Testamentary courts was usually, if not invariably, held by a clergyman. The father of these children, then, was a clergyman and a Master of Arts. We have record of only one Lawrence Washington to whom that would apply, namely the fifth (?) son of Lawrence Washington of Sulgrave, brother of Sir William Washington of Packington, and of Sir John Washington of Thrapston. He was student, Lector and Fellow of Brasenose, and in 1631 Proctor of the University of Oxford, and afterwards Rector of Purleigh. The long search after the true line of ancestry of our Washington, begun in 1791, was practically brought to a successful close when that little paper was discovered on Monday, the third of June, 1889.

My next object was to find out, if possible, how it was that Mr. Lawrence Washington became acquainted with people in Tring, what influences led him thither, and how he came to settle there or in its neighborhood apparently after his ejection from Purleigh in 1643. With that end in view I went to the British Museum and consulted the various Histories of Herts, by Salmon, Chauncy, Clutterbuck and Cussans, reading everything they had to say about Tring and the families seated in its neighborhood; and I made another interesting discovery, and one very much to the point. The manor of Pendley, which is partly within the parish of Tring and partly in the neighboring parish of Aldbury, but with its *caput manerii*, or manor house, in the former parish, held, 10 Edward I., by John d'Aygnel, and thence descending finally to the family of Verney, was sold by Sir Francis Verney to Richard Anderson, Esq., who held a court there, *Anno 5 Jac. I.*, and was knighted two years afterwards. Sir Richard Anderson's wife, Mary, was a daughter of

Robert, Lord Spencer, Baron of Wormleighton, owner of the manor of Althorp in Northampton, the great friend of the Washingtons of Sulgrave and Brington, as the old account books preserved at Althorp show* (see Col. Chester's paper already referred to). This was strong corroboration of the other evidence identifying this Mr. Lawrence Washington, if corroboration were needed, and it was also a complete answer to those questions which had been raised in my mind about the influences which brought Mr. Washington to Tring. This Sir Richard Anderson seems to have been by far the most important parishioner then living in Tring, where he died 3 August, 1632, and was buried within the chancel rail of the parish church. His widow, Dame Mary Anderson, afterwards lived in Richmond Surrey, but was buried at Tring, July, 1658. I examined the will of Sir Richard Anderson, and was gratified to find further evidence confirming my conjecture. It was as follows:

Sir Richard Anderson of Pendly in the county of Hartford knight, 5 October 1630, proved 27 August 1632. To the poor of Bitterly in Shropshire, Norton in Glostershire, Corringham in Essex, Albury, Tringe and Wigginton in Hartfordshire, to each parish five pounds. To the town of Tringe ten pounds to be added and employed, with that money already there in stock, to set the poor on work, which money of my own and some others given to that use is in ffeoffee's hands at this time thirty pounds. To my uncle Francis Garaway or, if dead, amongst his children, twenty pounds; to my uncle Mʳ. John Bowyer and my two cousins, his sons John and Francis, either of them, ten pounds. To my brother in law Mr. Thomas Cowly, now consul at Sante, twenty pounds.

Item I bequeath to Mr. Robinson's two sons, one of Pembrooke College, the other of Albourne Hall, and to my cousin Larance Washington of Brasenose and to Mr. Dagnall of Pembrock College, to each of them forty shillings.

To my wife (over and above her jointure) bedding and household stuff, belonging in my father's time to a house he had in Chiswick, &c. &c. My bigger diamond ring to my daughter Elizabeth. I will and bequeath to my dear and only surviving sister the Lady Spencer of Offley twenty pounds. To the Right Hon. the Lord Spencer, Robert Needham Esq., Richard Spencer Esq., Sir Edward Spencer knight and Sir Thomas Derham knight, my worthy brothers-in-law, ten pounds each. Provision made for second

---

* It seems proper to state that these extracts from the Althorp documents were first published in 1860 by Rev. John Nassau Simpkinson, then rector of Brington, in Northamptonshire, now rector of North Creake, in Norfolk. This gentleman being greatly interested in the supposed identity of the emigrants to Virginia with John and Lawrence of his parish, wrote a very pleasant story about the Washingtons, and appended many extracts from the household books of Lord Spencer. When Col. Chester utterly upset this theory, Mr. Simpkinson wrote a manly letter to the New York Nation, printed 15th April, 1880, acknowledging his mistake. Now, however, that the fact seems established that all the facts collected related to the father and the uncles of our Virginians, it is to be hoped that his book will again meet public favor. Very curiously in that letter Mr. Simpkinson refers to Col. Chester's collections which had been shown to him in confidence, and adds, "that some of these documents seemed to me to supply strong presumptive proof that the emigrants would be found, after all, to have sprung from the Northamptonshire stock, though of a generation below that which was erroneously pointed out." This hint makes one seriously doubt if Col. Chester were wise in declining to print his collections and surmises until he had full proof, and also to hope that these collections will no longer remain secluded from our knowledge until they shall have lost all value and interest by the independent researches of others.—W. H. WHITMORE.

son Robert and third son John, and two younger sons William and Richard (under one and twenty). Eldest daughter Elizabeth, second daughter Mary and third daughter Frances (all unmarried). To five younger daughters, Margaret, Katherine, Penelope, Ann, and Bridgett. Son Henry. My wife Dame Mary. The manor of Corringham in Essex. Cousin Henry Derham gent. Audley, 86 (P. C. C.).

Nothing could be better than this. Having found Mr. Washington at Tring, or in its neighborhood, I was now able to show through what influence he was led to go there.

Similar questions arose as to the connection of William Roades of Middle Claydon, Bucks, with Tring and its neighborhood, and the connection of the Washington family of Sulgrave and Brington with Middle Claydon; important questions if the hypothesis which I had assumed was correct, viz. that William Roades, Amphillis Washington, Susanna Billing and Elizabeth Fitzherbert, were all step-children of Mr. Knowling and children of -   Roades deceased, either of Tring or of Middle Claydon. Looking into Lipscomb's History of Buckinghamshire I found that the manor of Middle Claydon passed to the Verney family between 1434 and 1467, in which latter year it belonged to Sir Ralph Verney, knight and alderman of London. But this was the very family which held the manor of Pendley, in Tring and Aldbury, as their chief seat for so many generations until, as I have said, Sir Francis Verney sold it in 1607 to Sir Richard Anderson. The manor of Middle Claydon had been leased in 1535 for one hundred years to the Gifford family and from them to Mr. Martin Lister, who, in 1620, when the lease had but fifteen years to run, surrendered it to Sir Edmund Verney a brother of Sir Francis.

Here then was a promising clew to follow in order to get at the connection between Tring and Middle Claydon, and I thought it well worth the while to hunt for Sir Edmund Verney's will, which I soon found. The following is an abstract:—

Sir Edmund Verney of Middle Cleydon, in the co. of Bucks knight, 26 March, 14 Charles, A.D. 1639, proved 23 December, 1642. My body I will shall be interred in the chancel of the parish church of Middle Cleydon. To the poor of that parish twenty pounds. To my son Thomas Verney, for and during his natural life, one annuity or yearly sum of forty pounds payable quarterly. To my son Henry a similar annuity of thirty pounds. To my son Edmund and every of my daughters, Susanna, Penelope, Margaret, Cory, Mary and Elizabeth respectively, the sum of five pounds. To my cousin Edmund Verney, son of my uncle Urian, an annuity of five pounds, payable quarterly. To my niece Dorothy Leeke twenty pounds.

Item I do give and bequeath unto my servant John Roades of Middle Cleydon aforesaid for and during his natural life an annuity or yearlie sume of ten pounds of lawfull money of England to be paid unto him everie yeare for that tyme at the before mencoued foure fests by even porcons, The first paiefit thereof to be made att such of the said fests as shall first come and be next after my decease. To my servant Thomas Chauncy an annuity of five pounds. To my daughter in law Mary Verney, wife of my son Ralph Verney, forty pounds for the buying of her a ring. To my dear mother Dame Margaret Varney all such moneys as are, at the day of the date of this my last will, in her custody and which were not delivered by me or by my appointment unto her to make payment thereof for me. Certain other bequests to wife &c. Son Ralph Verney to be sole executor. William Roades one of the witnesses. Campbell, 129 (P. C. C.).

Can it be doubted for one instant that the William Roades, who witnessed the above will, was the very same person mentioned in Mr. Andrew Knowling's will? or that John Roades, to whom the annuity of ten pounds was left, was one of this family? Was it possible to learn anything more about them? The Camden Society published in 1853 some "Letters and Papers of the Verney Family, down to the end of the year 1639" (John Bruce, Esq., Editor). On page 208 I found that this John Roades was called Sir Edmund's bailiff at Claydon. In 1639 (1st April) Sir Edmund wrote from Yorke to his son Ralph, then at the family residence in Covent Garden, London, as follows : "I thinck my man Peeter and I am parted ; if he comes to Lundon bee not deceaved by any falce message ; wright privately as much to Roades." The Christian name is not given. On the 21st of June (1639) he writes from camp to his son : "I pray write to Will Roads presently to inquire out some grass for geldings, for I have bought fifty horses and geldings out of one troope, and they will bee at Cleydon about tenn dayes hence. The horses I will keepe att howse till I can sell them." What ever position John Roades may have held, it seems quite evident that in June, 1639, William Roades was bailiff at Middle Claydon. On the 25th of May, 1636, was issued a Warrant from Spencer, Earl of Northampton, Master of His Majesty's Leash, addressed "To all justices of peace, mayors, sheriffs, bayliffs, constables, and all other majesties officers and ministers to whom it shall or may appertayne," authorizing William Roads of Middle Claidon and Ralph Hill of Wendover, servants of Sir Edmund Verney, knight marshal of His Majesty's household, as deputies and assignees, for the space of six whole and entire years next ensuing, to take and seize to his majesty's use, and in his majesty's name, within all places within the county of Buckingham such and so many greyhounds, both dogs and bitches, in whose custody soever they may be, as the said William Roads and Ralph Hill shall think meet and convenient for his majesty's disport and recreation &c., and also to seize and take away all such greyhounds, beagles or whippets as may anywise be offensive to his majesty's game and disport.

Sir Edmund Verney was in his youth one of the household of Prince Henry. On the 7th of January, 1610–11, he was knighted. In 1613 he was taken into the household of Prince Charles as one of the gentlemen of the privy chamber. In 1622 he was appointed to the lieutenancy of Whaddon Chase, an office in the gift of George Villiers, then marquis of Buckingham and keeper of Wheddon, and an interesting letter to Sir Edmund from Sir Richard Graham, one of the Marquis of Buckingham's gentlemen, relating to this appointment may be found on page 106 of the Verney Papers. In 1623 he visited Madrid with other officers and gentlemen of the Prince's household, Prince Charles and Buckingham having already preceded them on that romantic expedition, undertaken for the purpose of seeing the Spanish infanta. In the service of the prince, as a page, was a Mr. Thomas Washington, whom Col. Chester satisfactorily identified as the sixth son of Lawrence Washington of Sulgrave and Brington, Lawrence, husband of Amphillis, being the fifth. The following extract from "Familiar Letters on Important Subjects, wrote from the year 1628 to 1650 by James Howell, Esq., Clerk of the Privy Council to King Charles I." (tenth edition, Aberdeen, 1713), becomes of interest to us. The letter was dated Madrid, August 15, 1623.

"*Mr. Washington* the Prince's Page is lately dead of a calenture, and I was at his burial, under a fig-tree behind my Lord of *Bristol's* house. A little before his death one *Ballard* an *English* Priest went to tamper with him: and Sir *Edward Varney* meeting him coming down the stairs of *Washington's* chamber, they fell from words to blows, but they were parted. The business was like to gather very illblood and come to a great height, had not Count *Gondamar* quasht it; which I believe he could not have done, unless the times had been favourable, for such is the reverence they bear to the Church here, and so holy a conceit they have of all ecclesiastics, that the greatest *Don* in *Spain* will tremble to offer the meanest of them any outrage or affront."

Thus we see that Sir Edmund Verney was intimate with one, at least, of the Washingtons and probably with others of the family, as two of them were for a time close neighbors to him, Sir William Washington, at Leckhampstead, and Sir Lawrence Washington, the Register of Chancery, at Westbury. And there was a connection of the Verney, Washington, Spencer and Fitzherbert families with the Leake* family which is yet to be unravelled. At any rate I think I have presented evidence enough to show how the Roades family may have been connected with Tring and Tring people, and how and where Lawrence Washington the student and Fellow of Brasenose may have made the acquaintance of his future wife. But the same evidence seems to show that it was a match which would not be likely to meet with the approval of the rest of the family, allied as they were to the Villiers, Sandys, Pargiter, Verney and other

---

* The father of Dorothy Leake, called niece in Sir Edmund Verney's will (often referred to in the family letters as Doll Leake), was Sir John Leake, son and heir of Mr. Jasper Leake of Edmonton. Her mother was Ann Turvill, daughter of Geoffrey Turvill, Esq., by Mary (Blakeney). As the widow Turvill afterwards became the wife of Sir Edmund Verney (the elder) of Pendley and mother of Sir Edmund the Knight Marshal, the Lady Ann Leake was the latter's half sister. I have yet to learn who the Penelope Leake was, whom Mrs. Elizabeth Washington of Brington called cousin.

families then of good social standing; and, in connection with this, it is worth noting that I have thus far seen no mention of Mr. Lawrence Washington in any of the wills of the family or their connections after this marriage, which must have been soon after the resignation of the fellowship (March, 1632-3).

I now went to the Public Record office and examined the exchequer: First Fruits, Bishop's certificates, Diocese of London (from April, 1630, to April, 1635), and looked over the "Names and cognomens of all and singular Clerks collected, admitted or instituted to any Benefice, &c., in the Diocese of London, and of patrons, &c., from 12 Sept. 1632, to 16 April," &c., and found the following:

Essex; Dengy, Decimo quarto die mensis Martii Anno preḋ Laurentius Washington clicus in Artibus magr̃ admissus fuit ad Rc̃oriā de Purleigh Cofñi Essexie per pñtaconem Janæ Horzmanden patronissæ pro hoc vice.

I also found in the book of compositions for First Fruits the following:

xll° die martii 1632 Anno Regni dñi nr̃i nunc Caroli Regis &c. octavo. Essex. Purleigh. R. Laurentius Washington clic comp̃ pro p'rmittis Rc̃orie preḋ ext. at xxv dec̃ia inde l'. Obligant' dctus Laurentius, Thomas Beale de Yorkhill in Cofñi Hereff geñ et Willūs Smith pochie bt̃e Marie de la Savoy Inholder.

This living he held until 1643, when he was ejected, by order of Parliament, as a Malignant Royalist. This information is given on page 4 of "The First Century of Scandalous, Malignant Priests Made and admitted into Benefices by the Prelates, in whose hands the ordination of Ministers and Government of the church hath been," published by John White and printed by George Miller, by order of Parliament, 17 Nov. 1643. The case of Mr. Washington is No. 9 on the list, and is as follows:

The Benefice of Lawrence Washington, Rector of *Purleigh* in the County of *Essex* is sequestred, for that he is a common frequenter of Ale-houses, not onely himselfe sitting dayly tippling there, but also incouraging others in that beastly vice, and hath been oft drunk, and hath said, *That the Parliament have more Papists belonging to them in their Armies than the King had about him or in his Army, and that the Parliaments Armie did more hurt than the Cavaliers, and that they did none at all;* and hath published them to be Traitours, that lend to or assist the Parliament.

In an account of the sufferings of the clergy, by John Walker (London, 1714), I found, in Part II. 395[b], the following remarks upon this case:

Washington, Lawrence, A.M., Purleigh R., one of the best Livings in these Parts: To which he had been Admitted in March 1632, and was Sequestred from in the year 1643; which was not thought Punishment enough for him; and therefore he was also put into the Century, to be transmitted to Posterity, as far as that Infamous Pamphlet could contribute to it, for a *Scandalous*, as well as a *Malignant Minister*, upon these weighty considerations; That he had said (then follows the extract given above in italics, beginning "The Parliament," &c.)

It is not to be supposed that such a Malignant could be less than a Drunkard; and accordingly he is charged with frequent Commissions of that Sin; and not only so, but with encouraging others in that Beastly Vice. Altho' a Gentleman (a Justice of the Peace in this County) who Personally knew him, assures me, that he took him to be a very Worthy, Pious man, that as often as he was in his Company he always appeared a very Moderate, Sober Person; and that he was Received as such, by several Gentlemen, who were acquainted with him before he himself was: Adding withal, that he *was a Loyal Person, and had one of the best Benefices in these Parts; and this was the Only cause of his Expulsion, as I verily believe.* After he subjoyns, That Another Ancient Gentleman of his Neighborhood, agrees with him in this Account. Mr. Washington was afterwards permitted to Have and Continue upon a Living in these Parts; but it was such a Poor aud Miserable one, that it was always with difficulty, that any one was persuaded to Accept it.*

We have here the two sides of the story. Whatever judgment we may form as to the charge of being "oft drunk" (which I myself am inclined to reject, or at least view with leniency), we can have no doubt as to his having been a plain and outspoken Royalist. We have the evidence of both sides as to that. How was it, now, with his kindred, friends and connections in that respect? So far as we can learn about them in the records, most of them were on the losing side, as well. To instance a few of them, we have seen that two of his elder brothers, William and John, had been knighted, which rather points that way; the former married Anne Villiers, half sister to the first Duke of Buckingham of that family, the Royal favorite. His eldest son, Henry Washington, nephew of the persecuted parson of Purleigh, was a Colonel in the Royalist Army, and, according to an account which I have seen, Governor of the ever loyal city of Worcester. He was called "late of the City of Worcester" in October, 1649, when he was obliged to "compound" for having been in arms against Parliament. Col. William Legge, who married Elizabeth, one of the sisters of the loyal Colonel, was a notorious Royalist, and endured great hardships on account of it. We have only to look through the Docket of the Signet office to

---

* I would here offer a criticism which Mr. Waters may have felt a scruple about making. Col. Chester, in his essay, after quoting this last paragraph, adds, "It is to be hoped that some further trace of him [Rev. Lawrence Washington] may yet be discovered in the neighborhood of Purleigh, where, *putting the usual construction upon Walker's language*, he continued in his profession of a clergyman after the Restoration, and consequently some years after the date of his namesake's emigration to Virginia."

It seems to me, that unless a number of instances can be shown from Walker's book, the usual *construction* would not at all imply that Washington continued to live and serve till after the Revolution of 1660. He was ejected from Purleigh in 1643; if he lived till 1653 or 1654, this would be such a "continuance" as would fully meet Walker's terms.

In fact, Col. Chester was so strongly convinced that Sir John and Rev. Lawrence were not the emigrants to Virginia (an opinion in which all our readers will now concur), that he seems to have over-stated Walker's language, in order to prove that Lawrence was in England after 1657, when his namesake was in Virginia. But it is more satisfactory still to find, as Mr. Waters does, that Rev. Lawrence was dead before 1655; for in a pedigree, as in politics, Stafford's merciless proverb is true, "stone-dead hath no fellow."

W. H. WHITMORE.

learn how he was betrusted and rewarded by his Royal master. Upon the Restoration, we are told, he was offered an earldom, but feeling unable to support that dignity, spoke in the interest of his son George, who, we know, was created Earl of Dartmouth. Sir Lawrence Washington, the Register of Chancery, actually died in Oxford, 1643, while it was held by the King's forces, having gone thither to attend the Royal Seal, as we are informed by Sir John Tirrell of Springfield, knight, who married Martha Washington, his daughter, and who was himself forced to pay a fine of eight hundred pounds in compounding for his own loyalty. Spencer, Earl of Northampton, whose grandfather had taken, for a second wife, one of the Spencer family of Althorp, and whose own mother was also a Spencer, of another branch, was one of the most distinguished of the Royalists, as were all his sons. He was mulcted most heavily for the part he had taken against Parliament, although an attempt seems to have been made to relieve his estates in Bedfordshire, by putting forward evidence to show that his agent collected the rents of these estates not for him, but as agent, really, of Sir John Washington, "by vertue of an extent wch the said Sr John Washington had upon the estate of the said Earle in the said County of Bedford." As to the Anderson family, we have seen that the kinsman and friend of our Parson was knighted. His son and heir, Henry Anderson, was created a Baronet by Letters Patent, dated 3 July, 1643 (see Chauncy's Herts), and we find that he also was obliged to compound for his loyalty in 1646.

I might extend this list, but I think I have given enough to show what the surroundings of our Washington family were in that respect; and I am quite sure I have seen enough myself to lead me to form the opinion that there was quite a nest of Royalists in that part of Herts and Bedfordshire, and I have little doubt that it was largely on that account that Lawrence Washington, the royalist clergyman, was led to seek that neighborhood and stay there. He must have died, as we have seen, before 1655. His wife was buried 19 January, 1654–5, and their children were thus left orphans. Their eldest son, John, was about twenty-three or twenty-four in 1657; for it is to be presumed that Mr. Washington did not marry until he had resigned his Fellowship in March, 1632–3 (according to Col. Chester), and Lawrence, we know, was twenty-two in 1657. Supposing them to have been young men of only ordinary enterprise and ambition, with the desire to get on in the world, what chance had they in England at that time, known as belonging to a royalist family, with all, or most, of their friends, to whom, in happier conditions, they might have applied for influence, royalists like themselves, and Cromwell then most firmly seated in his Protectorate? The chances would seem to be utterly against them. No wonder their thoughts turned to Virginia, that transatlantic haven and place of refuge for defeated royalists, which perhaps then first received the name by which it has, since, more than once been called, the home of the Cavaliers in America.

And though without influential friends to help them in old England, had they no good friends to start them in the new world? To this question I think I can give an affirmative answer. Their aunt Margaret, after the death of her first husband, Samuel Thornton, married again, into the Sandis family, one of whom is thus referred to in the following will:

NICHOLAS FARRAR, citizen and skinner of London, 23 March 1619, proved 4 April 1620. My body to be buried in the place where it shall please God to appoint. And for my worldly goods, first, whereas there is lately given a beginning to the erecting and founding of a College in Virginia for the conversion of Infidels' Children unto Christian Religion, my will is that when the said College shall be erected and to the number of ten of the infidels' children therein placed to be educated in Christian religion and civility that then my executor shall give and pay the sum of three hundred pounds unto the Company of Virginia, to be disposed of with the advice and consents of Sir Edwin Sandys, now Treasurer of the Company, and my son John Farrar, so as may most tend to the furtherance of that godly work of the College and thereby to the advancement of God's glory. And in the mean while until such time as the said College shall be erected and at least ten of the infidels' children therein placed, until which time I will not that the said three hundred pounds shall be paid or delivered by my executor unto the Company of Virginia, my will is that my executor shall pay and deliver yearly the sum of twenty and four pounds unto the hands of Sir Edwin Sandys and John Farrar, which said sum of twenty and four pounds my will and desire is the said Sir Edwin Sandys and John Farrar shall yearly pay by eight pounds apiece to any three several persons in Virginia, of good life and fame, that will undertake therewith to procure and bring up each one of the Infidels' children instructing them carefully in the grounds of Christian Religion and intreating them in all things so Christianly as by the good usage and bringing of them up the Infidels may be persuaded that it is not the intent of our nation to make their children slaves but to bring them to a better manner of living in this world and to the way of eternal happiness in the life to come.

Soame, 32 (P. C. C.).

This Sir Edwin Sandys, of Northborne (Kent), second son of Dr. Edwin Sandys, Archbishop of York, received the honor of knighthood from King James I. (says Burke), and was distinguished as a politician in that king's and in the subsequent reign. "He was (says an old writer) a leading man in all parliamentary affairs, well versed in business, and an excellent patriot to his country, in defence of which, by speaking too boldly, he, with Selden, was committed into custody, 16 June, 1621, and not delivered thence till 18 July following, which was voted by the House of Commons a great breach of their privileges. He was treasurer to the undertakers for the western plantations, which he effectually advanced, was a person of great judgment, and, as my author saith, *ingenio et gravitate morum insignis.*" He died in 1629.

Alice Washington, another of the paternal aunts of these young men, was married to Robert Sandys of London, eldest son of Thomas, brother of this Sir Edwin. The widow of their cousin, Col. Henry Washington, was, later, married to Samuel Sandys, Esq., another nephew of Sir Edwin. And Sir Edmund Verney had long before sent one of his sons, young Tom Verney, over to Virginia. So it is evident that there was plenty of influence which could be exerted in their favor to assist them in their Virginia scheme.

ADDITIONAL NOTES.

The following notes and abstracts, gathered during the past six years, all relate, more or less, to this family of Washington:

LAWRENCE WASHINGTON of Souldgrave in the Co. of Northampton, gentleman, 18 October 1581, proved 11 February 1584. As concerning my body, which, as it was made of earth, so must it return to dust and earth again, I desire therefore and require mine "exequitor" to cause the same to be inhumate and buried in the parish church of Souldgrave aforesaid, in the South Aisle there before my seat where I usually use to sit, according to his discretion. To Mr. Walter Light a whole sovereign of gold and to his now wife a "ducate" of gold. Towards the amending of Stanbridge Lane twenty shillings. And I will that Roger Litleford shall have the oversight in amending the said lane and bestowing the said twenty shillings. And for his pains in that behalf to be sustained I will him two shillings. And I will to every one of my sons' and daughters' children five shillings apiece, and to every one of my brother Leonard Washington's children six shillings eight pence a piece willed to them by Parson Washington.* Also I give to my brother Thomas Washington's children by his last wife forty shillings. Also I devise to my son Lawrence Washington one goblet parcel gilt, with the cover for the same, and four pounds of currant English money to buy him a salt. And I further will to him one featherbed in the gate-house, one feather bed over the day-house, one coverlet with a blue lining, one coverlet in the gate-house chamber, two boulsters, two pairs of blankets, four home made coverlets & four mattresses. Also I give to Lawrence Washington, son to Robert Washington my son and heir apparent, the ring which I usually wear. Also I forgive and acquit my brother Thomas Washington of all such debts and duties as he by any manner of means oweth unto me. And I forgive and discharge John Lagoe, sometime my servant, of all such sums of money as he oweth unto me and of all rents and arrearages of rents due unto me for such lands, tenements or hereditaments as he holdeth of mine, by lease or otherwise, for term of my natural life. And I will to every one of my servants which shall be in service with me at the time of my decease twelve pence. Also I will that the said Robert Washington shall yearly give to my servant Symon Wood a livery coat and forty shillings of currant English money for his wages yearly during his life. And whereas I stand charged by the last will and testament of William Bond, gentleman, for the amending and repairing of Preston Lane and for the repairing of the way between Dalington and the Westbridge at North-

---

* This may have been Lawrence Washington, junior, presented to the living of Stotesbery (Northampton) by Lawrence Washington, senior, 16 May, 1559 (see Bridge's Hist. of Northamptonshire, I. 203).

ampton called Spangstone, I earnestly require my executor and overseers to call upon the said John Balgoye for the amending of the said places, for that I have, long time heretofore, delivered into the hands of the said John Balgaye the sum of ten pounds of currant English money for the repairing of Preston Lane and twenty shillings for the amending of Spangston, for that only use and purpose. Also I will and devise that widow Compton shall have, hold, possess and enjoy for term of her life so much of one cottage as she now possesseth in Sulgrave, so as she well and honestly behave herself during her life, without making or doing any reparations thereupon and without paying any rent therefor, other than one red rose at the feast of Saint John Baptist yearly, if the same be demanded. And my further meaning and intent is that the said Robert and his heirs shall from time to time forever appoint some honest aged or impotent person to inhabit the same cottage for term of life, and that such aged or impotent person as shall not pay to my heirs any manner of rent therefor for term of his life other than a red rose payable as aforesaid, nor shall be charged to repair the same cottage during his or their lives. And my mind, intent and meaning is that if any doubt, ambiguity or controversy shall appear to arise or grow in respect of these presents then I will the same shall be decided and determined by my overseers or any one of them. And of this my last will and testament I constitute, ordain and appoint the said Robert Washington my sole executor, and of the same I make and ordain my well beloved and trusty friends the said William Baldwyn and William Pargiter my overseers, desiring them to call on my executor if any default or slackness shall evidently in him appear, for or towards the performance of this my last will and testament, and for their pains I will to either of them forty shillings. Witnesses, William Baldwin, William Pargiter, Robert Calcott, George Woodward. Brudenell, 5 (P. C. C.).

Northt. *Laurence Washington.*

Inq^n taken at Rothewell in Co. Northt 24th day of August, 26 Eliz. [1584] before Arthur Broke Esq. Escheator, after the death of Laurence Washington gent., by the oath of Henry Moore, William Craddocke &c. &c. Jurors, who say that Laurence Washington was seised in fee of the Manor of Sulgrave with the appurtenances to the Monastery of St. Andrew in the town of Northampton [lately] belonging; also of all the messuages, lands &c. in Sulgrave & Woodford to the same Monastery belonging; also of one close of land &c. [here follows a long list of lands in various places].

He being so seised by an Indenture made the 10th day of Dec. 7 Eliz. [1564] made between himself of the one part and Walter Light of Radwey in Co. Warwick gent. of the other part, in consideration of a marriage afterwards Solemnized between Robert Washington gent. then son & heir apparent of the said Laurence and Elizabeth Light then daughter & sole heiress of the said Walter Light, agreed for himself his heirs & administrators with the said Walter Light, his heirs & administrators that before the Feast of Easter then next following that he (Laurence) would make with certain persons indifferently chosen a firm and sufficient estate in two messuages in the parish of Pattishill with their appurtenances: to hold the same to the use of the said Laurence so long as the said Robert should live; after his death, to the use of Elizabeth Light for life, for her jointure; after her decease, to the use of the heirs male of Robert Washington; for default of such issue, to the use of the heirs male of Laurence Washington, younger son of the said Laurence named in the writ; for default of such issue then to the use of the right heirs of Laurence Washington (the father) for ever.

Robert Washington afterwards took to wife the said Elizabeth who is still alive at Sulgrave.

Laurence Washington (father) died on the 19th day of February now last past; Robert Washington his son & heir was aged 40 years & more at the time of taking this Inquisition.

The Manor of Sulgrave and other the premises in Sulgrave, Woodford & Cotton are held of the King Hen. 8, his heirs & successors in capite by the 20th part of a knights fee, and are worth per ann. (clear) £ 15. 12s. 6d. &c. &c.

Chan. Inqⁿ. p. m. 26 Eliz. Part 1, N°. 179.

WILLIAM PARGYTER of Grytworth in the Co. of Northampton, gentleman, 18 January, 26th year of the Reign of Elizabeth &c., proved 30 October 1584. To the church of Grytworth six shillings eight pence. To my son Christopher ten of my beasts, forty pounds of currant English money, after the expiration of one whole year, forty of my ewes that shall be going in my pasture in Stutesbury and forty of my store sheep that shall be going in the fields of Grytworth, to be delivered at any time, upon request, running out of the pen. I do release unto Richard Knight, my son in law, all debts whatsoever which he oweth me. To Ursula Knight, my daughter, one yearly rent of three pounds six shillings eight pence of currant English money, to be paid to her yearly by my son Robert, his heirs, executors or assigns, during the joint lives of the Lady Lawrence and of my said daughter Ursula Knight. To the said Christopher, my son, one dozen of pewter vessell.

"Item I doe give & bequeath unto my brother Wasshington his children fourty shillinges to be equally devided amongest them." To my sister Pemerton ten shillings. To my cousin Robert Manley his wife ten shillings. To my cousin Anne Crossewell ten shillings. To my cousin Anne Manley ten shillings. To every of the children of my son in law Crescent Buttery and Richard Knight the sum of forty shillings a piece, to be paid or delivered to them on the day of their marriages. To William, son unto Robert my son, my ring whereon my name is engraven. To Thomas Hancock ten shillings. To John Cowper my servant some of my apparell. To the poor of Grytworth, Laurence Marston and Sulgrave. The residue to son Robert, whom I make my sole executor. And I make and constitute my well beloved and trusty friends William Baldwyn, Walter Light, Robert Washington and Crescent Butterye, gent., overseers.

Watson, 31 (P. C. C.).

CHRISTOFER LIGHTE of Horley, in the Co. of Oxon, gentleman, 16 July 1583, proved 29 October 1584. To be buried in parish church of Horley under the gravestone where my father and mother were buried. My manor of Horley, my manor of Horneton, in Oxfordshire, my messuage and land in Mollington, Warwickshire, &c. &c. to my executors during the minority of Richard Lighte my son. My brother Walter, Johan Halford, my sister, and her children, vizt: Elizabeth Tyson and Ursula Halford. My cousin Robert Pargyter and Christopher Pargytor, and Ursula Knight their sister.

"And whereas I stande bounde by obligation to paye to my Cosen Robert Washington of Sowlgrave in the Countie of Northamptown gentleman, the Somme of one hundred poundes, yf I doe not suffer my Mannors, Landes and

Tenementes to discende unto him, my will is that my executors shall paye unto my saide cosen Washington his executors or administrators the saide soffie of one hundred poundes wthin one yeare nexte after my deathe in full satisfaction and pfourmance of the said Obligaçon, And in discharge of my promyse and agreement wth him made."

Wife Margaret. Five of the children of my sister Halford, viz: Thomas Savage, Elizabeth Tyson, Blanch Halford, Margaret Nicholls and Ursula Halford. I will and do desire my good brother-in-law Mr. William Pargytor of Grytworth, Northampton, and my well beloved brother Mr. Walter Lyght of Radwaye, Warwick, to be executors &c. My father-in-law Mr. Thomas Sheldon and my friend Mr. Ancar Brent to be overseers.

In a codicil the testator says " Whereas William Pargetor one of my exequitors hathe depted from this worlde longe sithence the makinge of my will I doe therefore nowe make and constitute Robert Pargitor, my kynsman, to be one of my Exequitors insteade of the sayde William Pargytor nowe deceased." Watson, 32 (P. C. C.).

Sir JOHN SPENCER of Oldthroppe, in the Co. of Northampton, knight, 6 December, 42^d Eliz: proved 11 January 1599. My body to be buried in the chancell of Bringhton Church, where my ancestors lie buried, and my funerall to be done in decent sort, not with great pomp according to the order of the world in these days. All my goods &c. to Robert Spenser my loving son whom I do ordain and make sole executor: and do ordain overseers of this my will my honorable good Lord the Lord Hunsden, Lord Chamberlain to the Queen's Majesty, and my loving and assured good brothers Sir William Spencer, knight, Thomas Spencer and Richard Spencer, Esquires, and do devise to them four of my best horses or geldings at their choice. To Lord Hunsden, further, one piece of plate, double gilt, of the value of twenty marks to be made in such sort as it shall seem best to my Executor. To my very loving friend Mr. William Baldwynne of Bifield, Northampton, twenty pounds in consideration of his care and pains in my law causes, and I will my son give him for me a good ambling gelding.

Also I will and bequeath unto Elizabeth Washington the wife of Robert Washington of Great Brinton, in the Co. of Northampton, in regard of her pains about me in my sickness, twenty pounds. To Agnes Fawkner my servant, over and above her wages, forty shillings. To Mr. Procter, parson of Bodington, five pounds or an ambling nag of that price, at his choice. And I give unto Mr. Thomas Campion my minister the presentation of the next Parsonage that shall fall, and if it be not to his contentment then to take that until a better do fall, and then to resign the worst and to take the best, the which I will and command my son to perform. I give to Stephen French and John Spencer, two of my servants that wait upon me in my chamber, forty pounds to each of them.

Kidd, 95 (P. C. C.).

ROBERT WASHINGTON of Souldgrave, in the Co. of Northampton Esq., 7 February 1619, proved 3 January 1620. My body to be buried in the South Aisle of the church before my seat where I usually sit under the same stone that my father lieth buried under.

I give to my three sons which I had by my second wife, namely to my son Albane Washington, to my son Guy Washington and to my son Robert Washington, the sum of one hundred pounds apiece of currant English money, to be paid unto them and to each of them at their ages of four and twenty years apiece, always provided, and I do mean, that my said three sons shall have the said sums of money aforenamed and at the time aforesaid if they be obedient and will be ruled in the mean space by their mother my executrix and do carry themselves well and as dutiful children to her, but if they, or any of them, be undutiful unto her and will not be ruled by her as it becometh them to be then I will by this my last will and testament that they, or so many of them as shall be undutiful or that will not be ruled by her, shall have but ten pounds apiece at their ages of four and twenty years apiece aforesaid.

Also I give unto three other sons which I had by my former wife, namely to my son Christopher Washington, to my son William Washington and to my son Thomas Washington, the sum of ten shillings apiece. And I do further give unto my son William Washington aforesaid the sum of fifty pounds to be paid unto him out of a debt of four hundred and odd pounds due unto me from the executors or administrators of my son Lawrence Washington deceased, and the said fifty pounds to be paid unto my son William Washington aforesaid as soon as it is recovered from the executors or administrators of my son Lawrence Washington as is aforesaid.

The rest of my goods and chattells unnamed and unbequeathed I give unto my wife Ann Washington whom I make sole executrix of this my last will and testament she discharging my last will and testament and discharging my debts and funerals.

Wit: Thomas Court, scriptor, Christopher Pargiter, John Ireton.

Dale, 5 (P. C. C.).

Of the sons mentioned in the foregoing will, Christopher and William entered Oriel College, Oxford, I think, in 1588, the former fifteen, the latter eleven, years old (as I learn from a memorandum furnished me by J. H. Lea, Esq.). The will or admon. of the son Lawrence, referred to, may be at Peterborough. I have not found it in London. He died at Brington, 13 December, 1616.

ELIZABETH WASHINGTON of Brighton (Brington), in the Co. of Northampton widow, 17 March 1622, proved 12 April 1623. I do give unto John Washington one hundred pounds and four pairs of my best sheets, two long table cloths, two pairs of pillowbeers and four dozen of napkins, four side board cloths, four cupboard cloths and four long towels, one put to drink in trimmed with silver, one silver beaker to drink in, one silver bowl to drink in, half a dozen of the best silver spoons and one double silver salt cellar, one pewter charger and a plate to it, six of the best platters and six dishes, a pair of andirons and tongs, a fire shovel, a chafing dish, a great brass pot which came from Solgrave, the best standing bed in the great chamber, with all that belongs to it, and half a dozen of Turkey work "quishions" and two long velvet "quishions" and a leather coffer. Item I do give unto Sir William Washington one hundred pounds. Item I do give unto Mrs. Mywse twenty pounds and one silver bowl and one brass pot. Item I do give unto Mrs. Alice Washington twenty pounds. Item I do give unto Mrs. Frances Washington twenty pounds. Item I do give unto my cousin Pill the bed wherein I do now lie, with all that appertains unto it. "Item I doe give unto my Cosen Lawrence Washington who is nowe at Oxford my husband's seal ringe."* Item I do give unto A:me Adcocke

---

* Qu. Did the sons of Lawrence Washington take this seal ring over with them to Virginia? If so, what became of it? Are there to be found any early impressions of it?

twenty five pounds, a pied cow and a pied colt and a yearling bullock, a great brass pott and two great deep platters and two pairs of fine sheets, one pair of pillowbeers and a dozen of napkins, a kettel and a dripping pan. Item I do give unto my cousin Penelope Leake who is now with me ten pounds. And of this my last will and testament I do make and ordain Mr. Francis Mewse my whole executor. And I do desire that all those dues and debts which is now owing by my late husband Mr. Robert Washington may be first discharged and then after them the legacies herein set down performed. And my desire is that my honorable good Lord Spencer would be pleased to be my supervisor of this my last will and testament.
Swann, 33 (P. C. C.).

The following monumental inscription at Brington is copied from Baker's Northamptonshire, Vol. I. p. 93:

Here lies interred y'e bodies of Elizab: Washington | widdowe, who changed this life for im'ortalitie | ye 19th of March 1622. As also y'e body of Robert | Washington Gent: her late husband second | sonne of Robert Washington of Solgrave in y'e | County of North. Esq. who dep'ted this life y'e | 10th of March 1622. After they lived lovingly together | many yeares in this Parish.*

Sir EDWARD VILLIERS, knight, Lord President of the Province of Munster in the realm of Ireland, 31 August 1625, proved 2 February 1626. I give and devise all my lands unto my dear and loving wife the Lady Barbara Villiers during her life, she to maintain and provide for my children. To my servant Hamond Francklyn two hundred pounds in one year after my decease. If both my self and my wife shall die without any issue begotten of our two bodies that shall be living &c. then my brother Sir William Villiers, Baronet, shall have all my lands &c., and he shall give unto my sister the Lady Elizabeth Butler one hundred pounds to buy her a jewell and to my sister the Lady Anne Washington the sum of five hundred pounds, and to every servant in my service at the time of my death one year's wages and to the poor people of St. Margaret's in Westminster the sum of twenty pounds. Skynner, 20 (P. C. C.).

PHILLIP CURTIS of Islip in the Co. of Northampton, gentleman, delivered his will nuncupative in the presence of Sir John Washington, knight, and Michael Westfield, clerk, 19 May 1636, proved 30 May 1636. To my daughter Katherine Curtis one thousand pounds, at day of marriage or age of twenty one, which shall first happen. Item I give unto my nephew John Washington the sum of fifty pounds to be paid unto him at his age of twenty and one years. Item I give unto my nephew Phillip Washington the like sum of fifty pounds to be paid at his age of twenty and one years. And for my nephew Mordant Washington I leave in trust to my wife. Item I give unto my wife Amy Curtis and to her heirs forever all my freehold land to be sold towards the raising of my daughters portion &c. And I make her the full and sole executrix &c. Item I make choice of Sir John Washington of Thropston, knight, and Michael Westfield of Islipp, clerk, to be guardians for my daughter. Pile, 55 (P. C. C.).

* This is one of the two "Memorial Stones" of which facsimiles were, in 1860, presented to Hon. Charles Sumner by Earl Spencer. Mr. Sumner gave these facsimiles to the State of Massachusetts, and they are now in the State House at Boston. The other stone is that of Lawrence Washington, brother of Robert, who was the grandfather of the presumed Virginia emigrants. He died Dec. 13, 1616.—EDITOR.

AMYE CURTIS of Islipp, in the Co. of Northampton widow, 27 June 1636, proved 19 November 1636. My body to be buried in the chancel of Islipp, near unto the grave of my deceased husband. I give towards the repair of the church of Islipp twenty shillings; to the poor there forty shillings: to the poor of Denford twenty shillings.

Item whereas there was given unto my nephew Mordaunt Washington, the eldest son of Sir John Washington, knight, by the last will and testament of his grandmother Curtis deceased the sum of fifty pounds to be employed as [in] the said will is further expressed my will is and I do give unto the said Mordaunt two hundred and fifty pounds more to be employed for his best benefit so soon as my debts be paid and the said money can conveniently be raised, and to be paid unto him at his age of twenty and one years or at the day of his marriage, which shall first happen. Item, whereas my husband, late deceased, gave unto John Washington, the second son of Sir John Washington, the sum of fifty pounds my will is, and I do give unto the said John my nephew the sum of fifty pounds more, to be employed for his best use and benefit, my debts first paid and the money conveniently raised, and to be paid to him at his age of twenty and one years, or at the day of his marriage.

A similar bequest to Phillip Washington, the third son of Sir John Washington.

To my god daughter Amy Hynde twenty pounds. To Michael Westfield, clerk, five pounds and to Mr. Richard Allen of Lowick five pounds. To my neighbor Mrs. Margaret Westfield five pounds. The freehold land given to me by my husband Phillip Curtis, I give unto my daughter Katherine Curtis. My mother Margaret Washington and my brother Sir John Washington to be guardians for my daughter.

Wit: Michael Westfield, William Washington and Phillip Freeman.

Pile, 108 (P. C. C.).

SAMUEL THORNTON, of St. Giles in the Fields, Middlesex, Esq., 9 January 1666, proved 2 May 1666. To my dear wife the sum of four hundred pounds, to my grandchild John Thornton two hundred pounds, to Charles Thornton my grandchild, one hundred pounds, to my grandchild Penelope Thornton one hundred pounds, to my daughter Kirby two hundred pounds, and I make and ordain my dear wife sole executrix.

Wit: Jo: Coell, Eliza: Mewce, Margaret Talbott.

Proved by the oath of Dame Margaret Sandis als Thornton his Relict & executrix named in the will. Carr, 41 (P. C. C.).

Will of Dame Margaret Sandys.

October the eleventh 1673. Into the hands of God the father, the son and the Holy Ghost, three persons but one eternal God, I do commend my soul, and I desire my body may be buried in a private plain decent manner. And that little I have I do desire should be thus disposed of. I do give to my dear sister Mewce twenty pounds and the hangings in our chamber and the silk blanket and my pair of sheets we lie in. I do give to my sister Washington, my sister Sandys and my sister Gargrave ten pounds apiece, which in all is thirty pounds. I give to my nephew John Washington, my dear eldest brother's son, twenty pounds. I give to my son Thornton my Indian gown. I give to my daughter Thornton twenty pounds and the hair trunk in my chamber and the linen in it. I give to my son Kerkby twenty pounds and my Turkey work chairs and the tables and carpets in the Parlour during his life and my daughter's, and after their deaths I give them to Lucy Kerk [Kerkby?] that waiteth on me. I give to my daughter Kerkby twenty pounds and my blue box in my closet and her father's picture in it and all else in the box. I give to my uncle Robert Washington five pounds. I give to young Lucy Kerkby that waits upon me ten pounds and the feather bed, bolster and pillows and blankets and three pairs of sheets she lies in and the wrought sheet and the chairs and stools in my closet and all my other things in my closet. I give also to her and her sisters my wearing linen and my clothes. I give to little Peg Kerkby my silver cup with the cover. I give to little Sam. Thornton my thirty shilling piece of gold. I give to little Nan Doman a broad piece of gold. I give Sam. Kerby a broad piece of gold. I give to the poor of Soham five pounds. I give to the poor of Fordham two pounds. And I make and ordain my dear son Thornton sole executor of this my last will and testament, desiring him to perform the same and those poor goods I have given that they may have them when I die and the money I have given that it may be paid to every one at the end of six months. In witness whereof I have hereunto set my hand and seal in the presence of the witnesses whose names are subscribed the day and year above written, and what money I have either here or at Haxey undisposed I give two parts of it to John Thornton and one part to Charles Thornton, my son Thornton's sons. And I desire my son that they may have it as soon as it is gotten but the charge of my burying must be taken out of the money I leave. MARGARETT SANDYS.

Wit: Do: Washington, Elizabeth Mewce, Lucy Kirkby.
Proved 16 November 1675 by Roger Thornton, the Executor.
Dycer, 118 (P. C. C.).

DOROTHY WASSINGTON, relict of Sir John Wassington, knight deceased, 6 October 1678, proved 24 December 1678. My body I leave to my executor's discretion to be laid decently in the grave in the chancel of the church of Fordham, near the place where the body of my dear grand child Mrs. Penelope Audley lies buried. And for that small estate which the lord hath continued to me I bequeath and bestow as followeth. Item I give and bequeath unto my son Mr. Thomas Kirkbey the sum of five pounds and to each of his sons and daughters twenty shillings a piece, to be paid them six months after my decease. Item all the rest of my goods whatsoever, as household stuff, bills, bonds, debts and the like, I give and bequeath unto my daughter Mrs. Penelope Thornton, whom I do make my sole executrix &c.

Wit: Ezech: Pargiter, Hugh Floyde, Sarah Flecher.
Reeve, 148 (P. C. C.).

The three preceding wills seem to show a confusion or mixing up of Sandis, Thornton, Kirkby and Washington. Dame Margaret Sandis was one of the sisters of Sir William, Sir John and the Rev. Lawrence Washington, and had been the wife of Samuel Thornton, Esq., before her marriage with ―――― Sandis. Dame Dorothy Washington was undoubtedly a daughter of William Pargiter of Gretworth, Esq., by Abigail, daughter of Sir Francis Willoughby of Wollaton, Co. Northampton, Bart. Her brother Theodore Pargiter's will (1654–1656) has already been published in these

Gleanings (Part I. pp. 84–5). I suppose the "Cosen John Washington" referred to in that will, apparently in Barbados,* was the second son of Sir John Washington of Thrapston, husband of Dame Dorothy. The following will of another brother of this Dame Dorothy Washington seems to prove the connection:

FRANCIS PARGITER of London, merchant, 10 January 1685, sworn to 28th and proved 29 October 1686. To the poor of the parish of Greetworth in the Co. of Northampton, where I was born, the poor of Westhorpe, adjoining to the said parish, the poor of St. Anne Black Friars (and others). To my sister Elizabeth Smith, widow, my sister Abigail Hickman, widow, my sister Phillis Pargiter, my niece Eleanor Pargiter, my nephew Edward Stratford, of Overstone, in the Co. of Northampton, Esq., my nephew Robert Stratford of Baltinglass in the kingdom of Ireland Esq. To such children of my niece Thornton as living, to such children of my niece Friend as living. To my niece Dorothy Marshall, widow, my niece Abigail Hickman.

I constitute and appoint my nephew Thomas Pargiter Doctor in Divinity sole executor of this my said will.

In a codicil, of same date, reference is made to a provision for the testator's nephew John Pargiter. Lloyd, 137 (P. C. C.).

The mention of the "children of my niece Thornton," evidently refers to Mrs. Penelope Thornton and her children (see wills of Dame Margaret Sandys and Dame Dorothy Washington). This I found confirmed by the will of Mrs. Mewce, a sister of Dame Sandys, as follows:—

ELIZABETH MEWCE in the Co. of Middlesex, widow, 11 August 1676, proved 12 December 1676. My body I commit to the earth whence it came, to be decently buried according to the discretion of my executors. I give and bequeath to my niece Mrs Penelope Thornton fifty pounds and my black shelf and my cabinet with all things that I shall leave therein. I give and bequeath to my niece Thornton's five children, John, Charles, Samuel, Roger and Dorothy Thornton, forty pounds. I give and bequeath to my sister the Lady Washington twenty pounds. I give and bequeath to my sister Mrs. Alice Sandys the sum of twenty pounds. I give and bequeath to my sister Mrs. Frances Gargrave the sum of twenty pounds and my clock and bed and hangings and sheets and all things to my bed belonging whatsoever. To my God-daughter Mrs. Elizabeth Sandys ten pounds. To my niece Mrs. Margaret Stevenage ten pounds and to her two children, William and Mercy Stevenage, five pounds apiece.

"Item I give and bequeath to my Uncle Mr. Robert Washington the Summe of five pounds:" to Mrs. Elizabeth Rumball, my niece, five pounds: to my nephew William Pill five pounds: to my niece Mrs. Frances Collins five pounds: to my nephew Mr. Robert Gargrave's five children, Robert, John, William, Elizabeth and Cotton Gargrave twenty pounds apiece and

---

* It may be well to note here that another of the name was in the West Indies. In Gov. Lefroy's elaborate book, "Memorials of the Bermudas," vol. 1, p. 384, he prints a document signed by eighteen of the inhabitants of Smith's Tribe, dated March 30, 1626. The fourteenth name is Laurence Washington.

Again, vol. i. p. 650, at a Council meeting June 20, 1649, "Mr. Axson, Washington and Bethell hayled to answer at next assizes for some words spoken against his majestie." This may or may not refer to the first-named Laurence. But clearly the Bermuda man was not our Rev. Lawrence, who was at this date at Oxford.—W. H. WHITMORE.

to Elizabeth Gargrave my silver dish and silver porringer and cup and two spoons and all the rest of my small silver things that my note speaks of. To my maid Anne Freestone thirty pounds and her bed that she lieth on, with all things belonging to it, and my suit of purple curtains and the other things in my rooms not mentioned.

I do make my two loving nephews Mr. Robert Gargrave and Mr. Roger Thornton executors of this my last will and testament, intreating them to take the care and trouble upon them, and I further desire these my executors, to let that money which I have given to my nephew Thornton's children be put into the hands of their trusty and loving uncle Mr. Francis Pargiter, merchant, to be improved for them till it is demanded, either to put the sons apprentices or for the daughter's preferment in marriage, &c.

Bence, 154 (P. C. C.).

Mrs. Mewce was another sister of Sir William, Sir John and the Rev. Lawrence Washington, daughter of Lawrence Washington of Sulgrave and Brington and widow of Mr. Francis Mewce of Holdenby in Northampton, to whom she was married, at St. Mary Le Strand, Middlesex, 26 May, 1615. I have not had time to ascertain in what way Mrs. Margaret Stevenage, Mrs. Elizabeth Rumball and Mrs. Frances Collins could be her nieces, nor have I succeeded in finding wills of her two surviving sisters, Mrs. Alice Sandys and Mrs. Frances Gargrave, who were also daughters of Lawrence Washington of Brington and therefore aunts of our presumed emigrants to Virginia. The uncle, Mr. Robert Washington, named in this will, as also in that of Dame Margaret Sandys, was, of course, the youngest son of Robert Washington of Sulgrave, Esq., by his second wife Anne (Fisher), and consequently a grand-uncle of the emigrants.

The pedigree of Mewce of Holdenby may be found in the Visitation of Northamptonshire, 1618–19; by which it appears that Mr. Francis Mewce was eldest son of Nicholas Mewce by Elizabeth, daughter of Edmund Morant of London, and had brothers Edmund and Christopher, and sisters Alice, wife of Richard Ellis of London, Lucy, Maline and Katherine wife of (Humphrey) Hawley of London. The following brief abstract is therefore worth preserving :

RICHARD ELLIES, citizen and haberdasher of London, 15 Aug. 1625, proved 26 Aug. 1625. Property in Rippon and Beverly, Yorkshire. Son Francis. Daughter Elizabeth. Reference to a bequest made to her by Mr. Nicholas Mewce. Daughters Ann and Mary and the child wife now goeth with. Sister Washington and god daughter Anne Washington. Children of sister Hyde, sister Croft, sister Vessey and brother Goderedge. Rev[d]. kinsman Mr. Jeremy Leeche. Aunt Gymber. Sister Hallye. Brother Humfrey Hally. Sister Malin. Brothers Mr. Francis Mewce, Mr. Edmund Mewce and Christopher Mewce. Clarke, 86 (P. C. C.).

Who the sister Washington is, who is mentioned in the foregoing will, I do not know.

The Lady Ann Washington, named in Sir Edward Villiers' will, was the wife of Sir William Washington, eldest son of Lawrence

Washington of Sulgrave and Brington, and therefore aunt by marriage to the presumed emigrants. She was a daughter of Sir George Villiers of Brooksby and half sister of the celebrated royal favorite, George, Duke of Buckingham. She was buried at Chelsea, 25 May, 1643. The following is an abstract of the will of her husband:

SIR WILLIAM WASHINGTON of Thistleworth in the Co. of Middlesex, knight, 6 June 1643, proved 1 March 1648. Whereas I am justly indebted unto Elizabeth Washington, my daughter, in the sum of twelve hundred pounds which she lent me in ready money and for payment whereof, at a time shortly to come, I have given her my bond of the penalty of two thousand pounds, my said daughter shall have and retain to her own use, towards satisfaction of the said sum, all that debt of eight hundred pounds, or thereabouts, due unto me upon two Obligations from the Right Honble William, Earl of Denbigh deceased, with the use that shall grow due for the same, and if any part of the said sum of twelve hundred pounds be paid and satisfied unto my said daughter in my life time, or after my decease, out of the overplus of moneys which shall or may remain due or payable unto me or my assigns upon the sale of my manor of Wicke and capital messuage called Wicke farm and other lands thereunto belonging which are now in mortgage to Henry Winn Esq. and John Chappell gent., redeemable upon payment of the sum of eleven hundred forty four pounds at a time now past &c. &c.

And my will and meaning is that, my other debts, which are not many nor great, being satisfied and paid in the next place, then all the residue of the money which shall remain and all my goods, chattles and personal estate whatsoever shall be equally divided amongst all my children that shall be living. And I make and ordain my said daughter Elizabeth sole executrix.

Wit: Rob: Woodford, John Pardo, Thomas Woodford, John Washington.

The will was proved by the oath of Elizabeth Washington *als* Legg, daughter of the deceased and executrix named in the will.

Fairfax, 29 (P. C. C.).

Sir William did not outlive his wife long, for the following entry may be found among the Burials in the Register of St. Martin's in the Fields, Middlesex:—

1643 June 22 Gulielmus Washington *eques auratus.*

From Col. Chester we learn that he was knighted at Theobalds on the 17th January, 1621-2, and that two of his children were baptized at Leckhampstead, in the County of Bucks., and two at St. Martin's in the Fields. The following are the two entries in the Baptismal Register of the last named parish:—

1618 November Susanna Washington.
1619-20 January 13 Geo. Washington fil. Gulielmi Washington gen^{si} & Annæ ux^r eius unius soror̄ p'nobilis Georgii Marchioñ & Comitis Buckingham.

One of the witnesses of Sir William's will was John Pardo; and I noticed, in the same parish, the marriage of Guy Washington and

Katherine Pardieu, 17 November, 1629. The bridegroom was probably Sir William's young uncle. I noticed too that a Richard Washington, gen., and Frances Browne were married, 27 April, 1627, and had children, Amata, bap. 21 October, 1628, and John, bap. 14 March, 1631-2. Richard Washington was buried 8 January, 1641-2, and Ralph Hall and Frances Washington were married, 17 January, 1642-3. A Philip Washington was buried 26 September, 1643.

Sir William's eldest, and, I think, only surviving son was Col. Henry Washington, the brave and resolute Governor of Worcester, for the King. He was buried at Richmond, Surrey, 9 March, 1663-4, leaving four daughters and a widow, Elizabeth, who was afterwards married to Samuel Sandys of Ombersley, Esq. One of the daughters, Mary Washington, of St. Martin's in the Fields, spinster, made a nuncupative will, 13 January, 1680, leaving everything to her mother, Mrs. Sandys, who renounced, with consent of her husband, and admon., with the will annexed, was granted to Catherine Forster, a sister of the deceased, 5 May, 1681. Abstracts of her will and that of her sister Penelope are given below :

MARY WASHINGTON, spinster, of the parish of St. Martin in the fields in the Co. of Middlesex, 13 January 1680, being in her last sickness whereof she died, with an intent and purpose to make and declare her last will and testament nuncupative and to settle and dispose of her estate, did utter and spake these words following, or the like in effect vizt: I desire that Hannah (meaning her maid-servant Hannah Lewis) may have one hundred pounds out of the money of the King's gift, and the rest I leave to my dear Mother (meaning Mrs. Elizabeth Sandyes), which words, or the like in effect she uttered and declared as and for her last will and testament nuncupative in the presence and hearing of the said Mrs. Elizabeth Sandys her mother, whom she desired to remember what she said to her, and of Katharine Hodges, Katharine Forster and Mary Hall and that she was at the premises of and in her perfect senses and understanding, the same being so done in the house of Mrs. Forster, her place of abode.

Letters issued 5 May 1681 to Catherine Forster, sister of the deceased, to administer the goods &c., for the reason that she had named no executor in the will, Elizabeth Sandys the mother, with consent of her husband Samuel Sandys Esq., expressly renouncing.   North, 83 (P. C. C.).

PENELOPE WASHINGTON of Wickhamford, Co. Worc. spinster, 6 December 1697, with codicil 5 January 1697, proved at Worcester 9 March 1697. To my niece Catherine Foster, spinster, two hundred and fifty pounds, but my mother and executrix, Madam Elizabeth Sandys of Wickhamford, to receive the interest of this money during her life. The said Catherine not to intermarry with any person without the consent of my executrix, being her grandmother. To my other niece Elizabeth Jollett (Gellett) the same sum on similar conditions. To my faithful servant Sarah Torey one hundred pounds. The residue to my said executrix.

By the codicil all the lands &c. in Bayton and elsewhere in Worc., conveyed unto me by Mr. William Swift deceased and his trustees, to " my deare mother Elizabeth Sandys" her heirs and assigns forever.

Seal—two bars, in chief three mullets.

The above will of Penelope Washington I had the pleasure of receiving quite recently from the Rev. T. P. Wadley, Naunton Rectory, Pershore.

In Add. MSS. 5705 (Brit. Mus.) may be found the substance of a petition from the four daughters of Col. Henry Washington, deceased "(transcribed from a book in the Surveyor Gen¹. of the Crown Land's Office, marked K. 1671–72 fol. 368 *ad* 372 inclu.)." They request a grant in consideration of the faithful service done by their father.

Mrs. Catharine Foster, sister of Mary and Penelope Washington, who administered on the estate of the former, was afterwards married to Barnabas Tunstall or Tonstall, of the Middle Temple, Esq., license being granted 9 March, 1686–7. She and her sisters are mentioned in the will of their aunt, Mrs. Susanna Graham, which follows :

SUSANNA GRAHME of Blackheath in the parish of Lewisham in the Co. of Kent 6 October, 1697, proved 30 March 1699. I desire my body may be interred in the parish church of Lewisham. To the Lady Dartmouth twenty broad pieces of gold which are sealed up in a paper with her name upon it. To my niece Mrs. Bilson ten broad pieces (as before) and the sum of one hundred pounds payable out of the arrears of rent which shall be due to me at the day of my death. Besides I give my said niece all the pictures in my little parlour at Blackheath, except my Lady Mordants. To my nephew William Leg Esq. one hundred pounds. To my niece Mrs. Dorothy Heron one hundred pounds. To Mrs. Penelope Washington five broad pieces of gold. To Mrs. Katherine Tonstall five guineas and to Mrs. Gelet, sister to Mrs. Katherine Tonstall five guineas. To my niece Mrs. Musgrave all my plate and china which I have in my house at Blackheath. To my Lord Preston all my furniture and household stuff at Nunnington, except my plate and china, which I give and bequeath to my niece Mrs. Susanna Grahme, his Lordship's sister. To the said Lord Preston his father's picture and my husband's set in gold. To Deborah Sanders all my furniture and household stuff in my house at Blackheath not otherwise disposed of. To my Lord Dartmouth two hundred pounds, out of the arrears of rent, and four hundred pounds which he oweth me, provided always that his Lordship in consideration of the said six hundred pounds settle upon the minister of the parish of Lewisham for the time being and to all future generations such a salary for the reading of prayers once a day at Blackheath as is agreed between us, and I beg and desire of him that the said salary may be so settled according to law that it may be firm to all future ages. To the said Lord Dartmouth all my pictures at Blackheath not otherwise disposed of, with my coach and horses, and five guineas to defray the charges of my funeral. And I constitute and appoint the said Lord Dartmouth sole executor of this my last will and testament.

Proved by the oath of William, Lord Dartmouth.

Pett, 40 (P. C. C.).

In the chancel of the old church at Lewisham, on a grave-stone of black marble, was this inscription : " Here lyeth | Mrs Susanna GRAHME | wife of | Reginal Grahme Esqʳˢ | Lord of this manor and second daughter of | Sir William WASHINGTON | who departed this life | the 26th day of February, Anno Domini | 1698 aged 81 years." This Reginald Graham was a citizen and draper of London, and belonged, I believe, to the royalist family of Graham of Esk and Netherby, in Co. Cumberland. He purchased, 23 May, 1640, of John Ramsay, Esq., the lordship and manor of Lewisham for £1500, and by deed dated 30 May, 1673, conveyed it to George Legge, afterwards Baron Dartmouth, as I learn from the new History of Kent, Hundred of Blackheath (edited by Henry H. Drake). Lord Dartmouth was eldest son and heir of Col. William Legge, a staunch royalist, who received license, 2 March, 1641-2, to marry Elizabeth Washington, of Kensington, Middlesex, spinster, about twenty-two, daughter of Sir William Washington, knight, of the same parish—at St. Faith's. Among the family letters is one of Col. Ed. Cooke to William Legge, Esq., Whitehall, dated Dublin, 10 January, 1662-3. He sends humble service to Legge's lady, his brother and sister Graham, Harry Washington, Dick Lane and all bedchamber backstair friends. Another, from Barbara, Lady Dartmouth, to Lord Dartmouth, 15 December, 1688, says: "it hath pleased God to take away your mother yesterday after a lingering illness . . . . she desired to be carried privately to the Minorits." One from Sir Harry Goodricke to Lord Dartmouth, dated York, 5 January, 1689-90, expresses the greatest affliction of his wife and himself at the irreparable loss of their dearest mother.

Col. William Legge, who had been a captain in Prince Rupert's Regiment, died at his house in the Minories, 13 October, 1670, aged 63, and was buried in the vault in the Trinity Chapel there, where also his widow was buried, 19 December, 1688, aged 76. Their grandson William, second Baron Dartmouth, was created Viscount Lewisham and Earl of Dartmouth, 5 September, 1711.

The following two or three abstracts refer to the Warwickshire branch of this family :

WALTER WASHINGTON of Radway, in the parish of Bishop's Itchington, in the Co. of Warwick, gentleman, being asked 1 January, 1596-7, by his uncle George Warner about the disposition of his estate replied that he would leave all to his wife and children. Commission issued 23 April 1597 to his widow Alice Washington to administer &c.

Cobham, 31 (P. C. C.).

Commission issued 18 September 1646 to Anne Washington, natural and lawful sister of Walter Washington late of Upton, in the Co. of Warwick deceased, to administer his goods &c.   Admon. Act Book (P. C. C.).

Commission issued, 18 September 1646, to Anne Washington, natural and lawful sister of Elizabeth Washington, lately of Tamworth, in the Co. of Warwick, but in Stepney in the Co. of Middlesex, singlewoman, deceased, to administer her goods &c.   Admon. Act Book (P. C C.).

ALICE WOODWARD of Stratford on Avon, 20 Aug. 1642, proved 22 May 1647. To be buried in the church of Stratford near late husband John Woodward gen¹. To the poor of Woodstreet Ward. To my son John Washington twenty pounds in six months. Bequests to grandchildren George, Elizabeth, Ann, Thomas and Katherine Washington, the children of the said John Washington, at their ages of one and twenty or days of marriage; also to grandchildren Thomas, Walter and Alice Stanton. Friend Thomas Nash Esq. Fines, 112 (P. C. C.).

JOHN DANVERS of Upton in the parish of Ratley in the Co. of Warwick Esq., 5 April 1658, proved 2 October 1658. My body to be buried in the parish church of Ratley. I give and bequeath my manor of Upton unto my brother-in-law Richard Swan, my brother George Danvers, my nephew Peter Yate and Ambrose Holbech the younger of Mollington, Warr., until my nephew John Danvers son of my late brother William Danvers deceased, shall attain his age of eighteen years; after that to my said nephew, with remainder to John Danvers, son of my brother George, then to my right heirs. To my brother Henry Danvers the income of five hundred pounds during his natural life, and after his death to Damaras Swann and Susanna Swann, daughters of my said brother Swann and of my sister Dorothy his wife.

Also I give and bequeath unto my brother-in-law John Washington the sum of one hundred pounds &c., and unto Anne Pepys, wife of John Pepys, of Littleton, in the Co. of Worcester, the like sum of one hundred pounds &c., and unto my godson John Washington of Kingston in the Co. of Warwick the sum of fifty pounds &c. (all payable within one year after the decease of the testator). Bequests made to Mary Yate, daughter of Peter Yate, to nephew Edward Yate, to Elizabeth, Hannah and Deborah, daughters of brother George Danvers, to Simon and Anna, children of sister Sibell Edulph, to Elizabeth Danvers, daughter of late brother William, to John and Katherine, the two children of late niece Katherine Goodwyn deceased, to God daughter Anne Tyler, daughter of niece Anne Tyler, to cousin Samuel Tyler and his wife and to brother Henry Browne and his wife.
Wootton, 449 (P. C. C.).

The testator of the above will was the eldest son of George Danvers of Blisworth, Co. Northampton, Esq., son of John Danvers of Cockthorpe, by Dorothy, daughter of Sir Richard Verney of Compton, both in the Co. of Oxford (see Visitation of Northamptonshire, 1618–19). His sister Anne (Danvers) was the wife of John Washington of Radway, son of Walter Washington, whose nuncupative will I have given. The latter's wife was Alice (not Catherine as in some of the pedigrees), daughter of John Morden *alias* Murden of Morton Morell, Warwickshire, by Katherine, daughter and coheir of Richard Marston of Draughton, Northamptonshire. After Mr. Washington's death, his widow Alice seems to have been married to John Woodward, who, I suppose, was the eldest son of Thomas Woodward of Butlers Marston (see pedigrees of Morden and Woodward in Visitation of Warwickshire, 1619). Katherine, daughter of Walter and Alice Washington, was married to Thomas Stanton, son and heir of Thomas Stanton of Woolverton

(Woolverdington), Warwickshire. A pedigree of this family is also in the Visitation of Warwickshire.

Commission issued 4 May 1612 to Anne Bateman *als* Washington and Lucy Cheesewright *als* Washington, natural and lawful sisters of Richard Washington, bachelor, in parts beyond the seas deceased, to administer his goods &c. Admon. Act Book (P. C. C.).

The above relates to a rather remote branch of the family, the said Richard, Anne and Lucy being children of Capt. Thomas Washington of Compton, Sussex (see pedigree). I now come to a nearer and better known line, which furnished a succession of Registrars of the High Court of Chancery, of whom the first was Lawrence, son of Lawrence and brother of Robert of Sulgrave.

License granted to Lawrence Washington and Johanna Sorrell spinster, of High Easter, Essex, to marry there, 16 July, 1576.

License granted to Lawrence Washington of Gray's Inn and Martha Newce, spinster, of Great Hadham, Herts., to marry there, 31 January 1577–8. London Marriage Licenses.

LAWRENCE WASHINGTON Esquire, Register of His Majesty's High Court of Chancery, 10 August 1619, proved 10 January 1619. I give, will and bequeath all my lands, tenements and hereditaments to my well beloved son Lawrence Washington, his heirs and assigns forever, and all my goods and chattells other than such legacies as I shall give and bequeath to my loving daughter Mary Horspoole, wife to William Horspoole, gent., and to any of her children, and to my loving brother Robert Washington and to my very good loving cousin Sir Justinian Lewyn, knight, and to the poor of the parish of Soulgrave in the co. of Northampton (and other legacies). I do constitute and make my said son Lawrence sole executor.
Soame, 3 (P. C. C.).

Funeral Certificate of Lawrence Washington, 1619.

Lawrence Washington of Maydeston in Kent gent. and Registrar of his Maties high Court of Chauncerie second sonne of Lawrence Washington of Sowlegrave in the County of Northampton gent. and daughter of William Pargiter of Gritworth in the County of Northampton aforesaid gent. deceased the 21 day of December 1619 at his house in Chauncerie Lane and was buried in the parishe Churche of . . . . in Maydeston in Kent aforesayd his body being thither translated on the 24 of the same moneth. He maried two wyves the first was Martha daughter of Clement Nuse of Haddam in the County of Hartf. gent. and had issue by her six sonnes and two daughters viz. Lawrence his eldest sonne and heire who also succeeded his father in the Office of Register maried to Anne Lewine the da. of William Lewine Doctor of the Civill Lawe and Judge of the prerogative Court, Clement his second sonne and Clement his 3^d sonne who dyed both without issue, Raphe 4 sonne, William 5 sonne, and an other all dyed before their father. He had also two daughters by the sayd Martha his first wife the first was Mary maried to William Horsepoole of Buckland neere Maydeston in Kent gent., the second daughter was Martha maried to Arthur Beswick sonne and heire apparant of William Beswick gent. of Spilmandine in the parishe of Horsemandine in the Countie of Kent aforesayd. The second wife of Lawrence Washington deceased was Mary the daughter of Sʳ Thomas Scott of Scotts Hall in the County of Kent aforesayd Knight and by her had no issue. This certificate was taken by William Penson Lancaster Herald the 14 of January 1619 and is testified to be true vnder the hand of Lawrence Washington the heire of the sayd Lawrence deceased.

Dr. Howard's Miscellanea Genealogica et Heraldica, 2d ser. vol. 1, p. 173.

Pedigrees of the Mewce family may be found in Berry's County Pedigrees (Herts) and in the Visitation of Hertfordshire (Harleian Society's Publications). William Horspoole and Mary Washington were married (by License), 27 May, 1602, at St. James Clerkenwell. He was son of Symon Horspoole, citizen and draper of London. (See Visitation of London, 1568.)

Commission issued the last of May 1647 to Simon Horsepoole, natural and lawful son of William Horsepoole late of Great Marlow, Bucks., deceased, to administer his goods &c. Admon. Act Book.

Sir JUSTINIAN LEWYN, knight, 8 July 1620, proved 11 July 1620. The land to descend to his daughter Elizabeth and the lady Elizabeth, his wife, to have the profits thereof during the minority of her child, towards her maintenance. The said Lady Elizabeth his wife to be his sole executrix. Ten pounds to be paid to the poor of this parish, ten pounds to the poor of Otterden. A hundred pounds to his sister Washington, fifty pounds to his sister Padgett, a hundred pounds to his sister Isam (Isham), a hundred pounds to his god daughter Elizabeth Huytt. Soame, 71 (P. C. C.).

SIMON HEYNES of Towerstone (Turweston) in the Co. of Bucks, Esq. 20 December 1626, proved 17 May 1628. My little nephew and god son Symon Heynes now in the house with me. As touching my freehold lands called Millfield, lying in Stuttesbury, Northampton, which I heretofore purchased of my cousin Lawrence Washington, of the King's Majesty's *in capite*, I dispose of two parts thereof in manner as followeth, leaving a third part thereof to discend to my son Henry Heynes according to law: one part to my wife, in lieu of her dower, and the other part to my said son for life &c. I make and appoint my wife executrix and my friends and kinsmen Lawrence Washington, Esq., and Simon Heynes, Esq., son of Joseph Heines, overseers.

The wife's christian name is omitted in the Probate.

Barrington, 40 (P. C. C.).

On a mural tablet on the south side of the chancel (Turweston) is inscribed the name of Simon Heynes, Esq., who died April 10, 1628.

Lipscomb's Hist. of Buck., III. 129.

Turweston is the next parish West of Westbury, some time the home of Sir Lawrence Washington.

Sir LAURENCE WASHINGTON of Garsden, in the Co. of Wilts, knight, 11 May 1643, proved 23 May 1643. To be buried in the church of Garsden. My daughter the Lady Tirrell. My nephew Simon Horsepoole. My servants Francis Cliffe, Allen Moore, Thomas Benson and William Freame. My son Lawrence Washington to be executor. To the poor of Garsden twelve pence a week for ever, to be bestowed in bread every Sunday morning, chargeable on my manor of Garsden.

(From the original will.)

The above will is one of the Oxford Wills (so called) which remain unregistered. The Calendars for 1643 and 1644 show many such. The Lady Tirrell mentioned in the will was Martha (Washington), wife of Sir John Tirrell or Tyrrell of Springfield, Essex, to whom she was married June, 1630 (see Visitations of Essex, II. 717). She died 17 Dec. 1670. Her husband was obliged to compound as a royalist in 1645, when he put in the following petition:—

"May it please this honorable Coffiittee to take notice that I was Sequestered for being at Oxford, & the occations of my goeing thither weare these—Sir Lawrence Washingtō my wife's father (haueing noe more children besides my wife & one sofie then under age) carried my wife frō my house att Springfield in Essex to his house at Garsden in Wilts that Midsoffier before the warrs began, & she being with child sent for me about Chrismas after, whereuppō I ρcured a Passe from the Lords & Coffions of ye Close Coffiittee to travell to her, & about Shrouetide after I got to Garsden, where the King Coffianded by his Garison in Malmsbury; soone after S^{ir} Lawrence went to attend the Seale at Oxford being ill before & at ye tyme of his goeing, but ye disease being quicker uppō him (for it began wth a gentle flux) & his sonne lying there also desperately sick, & his man sending m[e] word he spake of my coffiing, for ye settleing his Estate by deed (wch accordingly he did) uppō his sonne & after, uppō his daughter; I went to Oxford, where S^{ir} Lawr. shortly after died & his sonne hardly escaped, & then I returned to Garsden. Then my wife being sick at ye Bath & haueing spent o^r monys, I went shortly after to Bracly to my Tenant; & then ρcureing a Passe frō my L: of Essex I came to Londō last January was twelue months & found my estate sequestered & soone after my goods & stock weare sold; & I attended the L: & Coffions of ye honor^{ble} Coffiittee for Sequestratiōs till I was heard, & after, aboad in Londō till Mich: last when haueing no means longer to subsist I repaired to Springfield in Essex to my wife & childrē, where I aboad till about 3 weeks since.

I gaue 10£ to the first Propositions. I have payd the 5th & 20th ρt to the full, as appears by Certificate of ye Coffiittee at Chelmisford. I haue taken ye National Covenant. I have payd all Rates without distresse, before I was sequestred; & [ ] except 50£ to Habberdashers Hall last Mich: for 20th ρt wch I hope I am [ ] that my Certeficate saith I haue payd to the Full. My goods haue been sold & stock. My estate in Northamtōsheire lost & utterly spoyled. I had a Passe to goe into ye K: Quarters, & was at Ox: before or when the Ordenance for Sequestratiōs bears date; the occatiō was a greate Concerne unto me, to wit ye settleling Sir Lawr. whole estate by intaile; And my owne land near Bracley. I never boar Arams; nor assisted ye K: Nor kissed his hand whilest I was there."

"Yr humble Servant " Jo: Tirell"

"24o April: 1645."

The following inscription was copied at Garsden by J. Henry Lea, Esq.:

"To the Memory of Sʳ Laurence Washington Kᵗ lately chiefe Register of the Chauncery of known Pyety of Charity exemplarye A louinge Husband A tender Father A bountifull Master A Constant Relieuer of the Poore and to those of this Parish A perpetuall Benefactour Whom it pleased God to take unto his Peace from the fury of the insuing Warrs Oxon Maii 14ᵗᵒ Here interred 24ᵗᵒ Año Dñi 1643° Aetat Suæ 64° Where also lyeth Dame Anne his wife who deceased Junij 13ᵗᵒ and was buried 16ᵗʰ Año Dñi 1645."

> " Hic Patrios cineres curauit filius Urna
> Condere qui tumulo nunc jacet Ille pius.
> The pious Son his Parents here interred
> Who hath his share in Urne for them prepar'd."

Dame Anne Washington, his wife, was a daughter of William Lewin of Otterden, Kent, D.C.L., and sister of Sir Justinian Lewin, an abstract of whose will has been given.

LAWRENCE WASHINGTON of Garsdon in the Co. of Wilts, Esq., 14 January 1661, proved 15 May 1662. My body to be buried in the chancel of the Parish church of Garsdon. To the poor of Garsdon ten pounds, to be distributed to householders by five shillings to a house, and to the poor of Westamsbury and Bulford, Wilts, ten pounds &c.

"Alsoe I doe giue and devise vnto my Cozen John Washington sonne of Sir John Washington of Thrapston in the Countie of Northampton knᵗ one Annuitie or yearely Rent of ffortie pounds of Currant English money ffor and dureinge the terme of his naturall life To be issueing and goeing forth out of all my messuages Lands Tenements and Hereditaments and ffarme in Westamsbury alʲ Littleamsbury in the Countie of Wiltes aforesaid To be paid unto him at the ffeasts of Thanunciation of the blessed Virgin St Mary and St Michaell Tharchangell by euen and equall portions the ffirst payment thereof to beginne and to be made at the ffirst of the said ffeasts which shall happen come and be next after my decease and if and as often as it shall happen the said yearely Rent of ffortie pounds to be behinde and unpaid by the space of Tenne dayes next after any of the said ffeasts in the which as aforesaid the same ought to be paid that then and soe often it shall be lawfull to and for the said John Washington into the said Messuages Lands Tenements and hereditaments to enter and distreyne and the distresse and distresses then and there had found and taken to lead driue take and carry away and the same to impound deteyne and keepe untill the said Annuity or yearely rent of fforty pounds and all the arreares thereof (if any be) shall be unto my said Cozen John Washington fully satisfied and paid."

To Charles Tyrrell, youngest son of Dame Martha Tyrrell of Herne House in the Co. of Essex, one annuity of twenty pounds &c. To my cousin Symon Horsepoole of London, gent., one annuity of thirty pounds &c. To my beloved sister Dame Martha Tyrrell twenty pounds to buy her a ring, and to my nephews John, Thomas and Charles Tyrrell ten pounds apiece and to my niece Martha Tyrrell twenty pounds, to buy each of them a ring. To John Elton of Tedbury, Glouc., physician, for his great care and pains towards me and my family for several years past, forty pounds. To servants (not named). The residue unto Elianor, my wife, whom I make sole executrix &c.   Laud, 73 (P. C. C.).

Dame ELIANOR PARGITER, the relict of Sir William Pargiter late of Gretworth, knight, deceased, 17 July 1685, proved 2 June 1687. My body I desire may be carried in a decent and private way to Garsden in Wiltshire and interred there by my former husband Lawrence Washington Esq'. I will and bequeath to my dearly beloved daughter Ferrars my necklace of pearl, being two strings of pearl, which her father gave to me, one saphire ring, which he likewise gave to me, and her father's picture set in gold. To the parish of Garsdon thirty pounds, to be bestowed in decent plate for the Communion Table there, to be kept by the Minister of the place for the time being. To the poor of that parish ten pounds. The residue to my daughter Elianor Pargiter, whom I make, constitute and ordain sole executrix.

Proved by the oath of Elianor Dering *als* Pargiter.

Foot, 82 (P. C. C.).

She was the second daughter of William Guise of Elmore, Gloucestershire. She died 19 July, 1685, according to the monumental inscription at Garsden. Her first husband, Lawrence Washington, Esq., died 17 January, and was buried 11 February, 1661-2.

THOMAS POPE of the parish of St Philip and Jacob in Bristol, merchant, 3 September, 1684, proved 20 October 1685. Being now bound on a voyage to sea &c. To my wife Joanna, for and during her natural life, my messuage and tenement called Noble's corner, and all the lands and appurtenances thereunto belonging, situate in Barton Regis in the County of Glouc. The reversion and inheritance of the same messuage &c. I give and devise to my two sons, Charles Pope and Nathaniel Pope, their heirs and assigns, forever, equally between them as tenants in common.

Item I give and devise to my son Thomas Pope and the heirs of his body lawfully to be begotten all that my plantation, with the lands, servants, cattle, stock and appurtenances thereunto belonging, situate and being at or near Pope's Creek in Westmoreland in Virginia, with remainder to sons Charles and Nathaniel in common . . . My other plantation, commonly called Clift's Plantation, in Westmoreland, on the Potomac River, in Virginia &c. I give and devise to my two sons Richard and John Pope, their heirs and assigns forever. But my wife Joanna shall hold and be endowed of one third part of both my said plantations &c. for the term of her natural life.

Item I make my loving friends and kinsmen Mr. William Hardridge, Mr. Lawrence Washington and Mr. John Washington, all of Virginia aforesaid, and the survivors and survivor of them, guardians and guardian of my said sons Thomas, Richard, John, Charles and Nathaniel for the managing of my said plantations and premises in Virginia. They shall receive and take the rents, issues and profits thereof until my said sons shall attain their respective ages of one and twenty years, and they shall, from time to time, ship and consign the proceeds thereof to my said wife in England during her life, and, in case of her decease, to such other person or persons as shall be guardian or guardians of all or any my children, sons or daughters, to be by her or them from time to time disposed and laid out for and towards the better maintenance and education of all and every my said children.

I make, ordain and appoint Richard Gotley and Charles Jones the younger, merchants of the city aforesaid, executors in trust &c. And to each of my executors and to each of my above named friends and trustees in Virginia I give twenty shillings apiece as tokens of my love. Provision made for three daughters, Mary, Elizabeth and Margaret out of the personal estate (they under twenty-one).

Wit: John Churchman, Wm Meredith, Wm Brayne and John Selwood.

Cann, 124 (P. C. C.).

The Honorable JOHN CUSTIS Esq. of the City of Williamsburg and County of James City in the Colony of Virginia, 14 November 1749, proved at London 19 November 1753. My executor to lay out and expend, as soon as possible after my decease, out of my estate, the sum of one hundred pounds sterling to buy a handsome tombstone of the best durable white marble, large and built up of the most durable stone that can be purchased, for pillars, very decent and handsome to lay over my dead body, engraved on the tombstone my coat of arms, which are three parrots, and my will is that the following inscription may be also handsomely engraved on the said stone vizt.

"Under this Marble Stone lyes the Body of the Honourable John Custis Esquire of the City of Williamsburgh and parish of Bruton formerly of Hungars Parish on the Eastern Shoar of Virginia and County of Northampton the place of his Nativity Aged .... years and yet lived but seven years which was the space of time he kept a Batchelors House at Arlington on the Eastern Shoar of Virginia this Inscription put on this Stone by his own possitive Orders."

And I do desire and my will is and I strictly require it that as soon as possible my real dead body, and not a sham coffin, be carried to my plantation on the Eastern Shore of Virginia, called Arlington, and there my real dead body be buried by my Grandfather the Honble John Custis Esquire where a large walnut formerly grew and is now enclosed with a brick wall, which brick wall it is my will and I strictly charge and require it that the said brick wall be always kept up in good repair very handsomely by my heir that shall enjoy my estate; and if my heir should "ingratefully" or obstinately refuse or neglect to comply with what relates to my Burial in every particular then I bar and cut him off from any part of my estate, either real or personal, and only give him one shilling sterling, and in such case I give my whole estate, real and personal, to the next heir male of my family named Custis that will religiously and punctually see this my will performed, but more especially what any ways relates to my burial in general, and if by any accident the Tombstone and appurtenances should be lost, broke or any ways miscarry in coming in from England, or any other ways whatsoever, in that case my positive will is and I earnestly require it that my heirs or executors immediately send to England for such another stone exactly, with the appurtenances, of the same price, until one shall come safe to hand according to my will and desire.

I give to my dear friend Thomas Lee Esquire, if living at my death, two hundred pounds to buy him any one thing he has a mind to remember me. To my worthy and much esteemed friend John Blair Esq. one hundred pounds, and to Mrs. Mary Blair, his wife, five guineas to buy her a mourning ring.

Whereas my plantation called Arlington, on the Eastern Shore of Virginia is entailed by my Grandfather, the Hon. John Custis Esq., on the heirs male of my body lawfully begotten and for as much as my father, the late Hon. John Custis Esq., had a patent in his own name for two hundred and fifty acres of the said Arlington plantation which my said father has given me by his said will in fee simple, I do entail the said two hundred and fifty acres of land, so given to me, exactly in the same manner as the other three hundred acres contiguous or adjoining to it, and my will is that it always descend exactly in the same manner as Smith's Island and Motton Island, which are firmly entailed on the Heirs male of my body lawfully begotten by the will of my grandfather &c.

And whereas by my deed of Manumission recorded in the County Court of York I have freed and set at liberty my negro boy christened John, otherwise called Jack, born of the body of my slave Alice, now I do hereby ratify and confirm the said deed of Manumission unto the said John otherwise called Jack, and after the death of said John, otherwise called Jack, I give all the estate by me heretofore given to the said John, otherwise called Jack, either by deed or otherwise, to my son Daniel Park Custis to hold to him my said son from and after the death of the said John, otherwise called Jack &c. My will and desire is that as soon as possible after my decease my executor build on the said land I bought of James Morris, situate near the head of Queen's Creek in the co. of York, for the use of the said John, otherwise called Jack, a handsome, strong, convenient dwelling house according to the dimensions I shall direct, and a plan thereof drawn by my said friend John Blair Esq., and that it be completely finished within side and without, and when the house is completely finished it is my will that the same be furnished with one dozen high Russia leather chairs, one dozen low Russia chairs, a Russia leather couch, good and strong, three good feather beds, bedsteads and furniture and two good black walnut tables. I desire that the houses, fencing and other appurtenances belonging to the said plantation be kept in good repair and so delivered to the said John, otherwise called Jack, when he shall arrive to the age of twenty years. I also give him when he shall arrive to that age a good riding horse and two young able working horses. I give to Mrs. Ann Moody, wife of Matthew Moody, if she be living at my death, twenty pounds, to be paid her annually during her natural life. I also give her the picture of my said Negro boy John. It is my will and desire that my said Negro boy John, otherwise called Jack, live with my son until he be twenty years of age, and that he be handsomely maintained out of the profits of my estate given him. I give and devise unto John Cavendish, for the many services he has done me, the house and lot where he now lives to hold the same rent free during his natural life.

All the rest, residue and remainder of my estate, real and personal, be it of what nature or kind soever, or wheresoever lying and being in the whole world, I give, devise and bequeath unto my son Daniel Park Custis to hold to him, his heirs and assigns forever. And I do constitute and appoint my said son whole and sole executor. Wit: Thomas Dawson, George Gilmer, John Blair, jun^r.

The above will was proved at a court held for James City County 9 April 1750, Ben. Waller being Clerk of the Court.

On the twenty third day of Sept. 1784 Admōn. (with the will annexed) of the goods &c left unadministered by Daniel Parke Custis deceased &c., was granted to Wakelin Welch, the lawful attorney of Martha Washington, formerly Custis (wife of his Excellency the Honorable George Washington) the relict and administratrix of the rest of the goods of the said Daniel

Parke Custis deceased, for the use and benefit of the said Martha Washington, formerly Custis, now residing at Virginia aforesaid, the said Daniel Parke Custis dying intestate. Searle, 287 (P. C. C.).

Facing this page will be found a folded tabular pedigree which I have compiled to illustrate this article.

[Others of the name Washington than the famed brothers John and Lawrence Washington appear in the annals of Virginia:

"Robert Washington of Wapping in ye p'sh of Stepney and Town of Middlesex, Mariner," executed power of attorney to "Wm Pearson, Chirurgeon," "29th July 1660."

"Edward Washington, convicted of manslaughter and ordered to be burnt in the hand" October 12, 1675. *Records of General Court of Va.*

The following grants are of record in the State Land Registry:

Major John Washington, Book No. 5, p. 38, 320 acres in Westmoreland Co., M'ch 23, 1664. Major John Washington and Thomas Pope, No. 5, p. 49, 50 acres in Westmoreland Co., Sept. 4, 1667. Major John Washington, No. 5, p. 49, 300 acres in Northumberland Co., June 1, 1664; p. 50, 1700 acres in Westmoreland Co., March 26, 1664. Mrs. Ann Pope alias Washington, No. 5, p. 52, 700 acres in Westmoreland Co., June 13, 1661. Major John Washington and Thomas Pope, No. 5, p. 54, 1200 acres in Westmoreland Co., Sept. 4, 1661. Lt. Col. John Washington, No. 6, p. 349, 450 acres in Northumberland Co., Oct. 10, 1670. Lawrence Washington and Robert Richards, No. 6, p. 60, 700 acres in Stafford Co., Sept. 27, 1667. Lt. Col. John Washington, No. 6, p. 615, 5000 acres in Stafford Co., 1677; p. 183, 560 acres in Rappahannock Parish, Nov. 3, 1673. Richard Washington, No. 8, p. 165, 330 acres in Surrey Co., April 29, 1682; p. 464, 200 acres in Surrey Co., April 20, 1685; p. 88, 772 acres in Surrey Co., Oct. 23, 1690; No. 9, p. 326, 345 acres in Surrey Co., April 25, 1701. John and Arthur Washington, No. 9, p. 371, 742 acres in Surrey Co., 1701.

Neither Robert, Edward, Richard, John or Arthur Washington, appear to have been of the family of John and Lawrence Washington, from the records preserved of these brothers.—R. A. BROCK.

The *Daily Reporter*, Northampton, Eng., August 24, 1889, contains a description of the Washington Slab in Sulgrave Church, and an account of its mutilation about a fortnight before that date by two strangers in gentlemanly attire.

The Washington slab is thus described in the Northampton *Reporter*. Six different brass plates were let into it. The first contained the Washington coat of arms, Argent, two bars gules, in chief three mullets of the second. On each side, in brass, were "effigies of Washington and his wife, and below them on a brass plate of oblong form was the following inscription in three lines:

Here lyeth buried ye bodys of Laurence Wasshingtō Gent & Amee his | wyf by whome he had issue iiij sons & vij daughts w^o laurence Dyed ye day of | an^o 15 & Amee Deceassed the VI day of October an^o Dñi 1564. |

Under this are representations of the four sons and seven daughters in two groups.

The costume of Lawrence Washington and his children is that of the ordinary attire of civilians of the middle of the 16th century. The father wears a close-fitting doublet, a large loose gown, with demi-canon sleeves purfled with fur, and large broad-toed shoes. The boys wear large doublets, knee breeches, long hose, and shoes like their father; and each has his gyficière at his girdle. The girls wear close-fitting caps, with gowns reaching to the ankles, and secured round the waist with a band. The brass representing Amy Washington no longer remains. . . . Time has told somewhat on this monument of Lawrence and Amy Washington; and it is also to be regretted, the hand of the thief as well. The head of Lawrence Washington has been knocked off; the brass effigy of his wife has

HERE·LIETH·THE·BODI·OF·LAVRENCE
WASHINGTON · SONNE · & · HEIRE · OF
ROBERT·WASHINGTON · OF · SOVLGRAE
IN · THE · COVNTIE · OF · NORTHAMPTON
ESQVIER · WHO · MARIED · MARGARET
THE · ELDEST·DAVGHTER·OF·WILLIAM
BVTLER · OF · TEES · IN · THE · COVNTIE
OF · SVSSEXE · ESQVIER ·WHO·HAD·ISSV
BY · HER · 8 · SONNS · & · 9 · DAVGHTERS
WHICH · LAVRENCE · DECESSED · THE · 13
OF·DECEMBER·A : DÑI : 1616

THOV·THAT·BY·CHANCE·OR·CHOYCE
OF·THIS·HAST·SIGHT
KNOW·LIFE·TO·DEATH·RESIGNES
AS·DAYE·TO·NIGHT
BVT·AS·THE·SVNNS·RETORNE
REVIVES·THE·DAYE
SO·CHRIST·SHALL·VS
THOVGH·TVRNDE·TO·DVST·&·CLAY

been stolen and taken away bodily; and the enamel with which the coat of arms was colored has crumbled nearly all away, leaving scarce a trace behind. The two portions recently taken away are those representing the 'iiij sons and vij daughters.' Each of these pieces could be covered by a sheet of note-paper."

It is to be hoped that the perpetrators of this dastardly act may be discovered. An abstract of the will of Lawrence Washington and an inquisition post mortem are printed, *ante*, pp. 24–26.

Lawrence Washington of Sulgrave, grandson of Lawrence and Amee Washington, died Dec. 13, 1616, and was buried at Brington. In 1860, as has been stated in the foot-note on page 29, Earl Spencer presented to Hon. Charles Sumner facsimiles of two Washington memorial stones in the church at Brington, which facsimiles Mr. Sumner presented to the State of Massachusetts. One of these stones was that of this Lawrence Washington and the other that of his brother Robert. The inscription on the stone of Robert Washington and his wife Elizabeth is printed on page 29, from Baker's Northamptonshire. Mr. David Pulsifer, in the appendix to his edition of Rev. C. H. Wharton's Poetical Epistle to George Washington (Boston, 1881), gives an account of the presentation of the facsimiles to the State by Mr. Sumner. This account is accompanied by engravings of the two stones. Mr. Pulsifer has loaned us the cut of Lawrence Washington's stone, containing besides the inscription the arms of Washington impaling Butler; and it is printed on the opposite page. Lawrence and Margaret (Butler) Washington were parents of Lawrence Washington, M.A., rector of Purleigh, who, it is believed, was the father of the Virginia emigrants.—EDITOR.

CONCLUSIONS.

A careful examination of the preceding pages will doubtless bring the reader to the conclusion that Mr. Waters has made out a pedigree in the highest degree probable, and lacking absolute certainty only on the two following points. First, having shown that Lawrence Washington of Virginia owned land in Luton, we lack *positive* proof to identify him with the Lawrence baptized at Tring in 1635.

Second, having rendered it almost absolutely certain that the father of the Washington children baptized at Tring, was a clergyman and M.A., we lack *absolute* certainty that he was identical with the Rector of Purleigh.

On both these points we may hopefully expect assistance from our English friends, now that the field of investigation is so contracted. It may be fairly added, that whilst legal evidence on these two points is lacking, the industry and acuteness of Mr. Waters are signally shown in the great amount of circumstantial evidence by him collected, which indeed affords us a moral certainty of the entire correctness of the pedigree.

It is a curious fact that the first pedigree as drawn up by Sir Isaac Heard, should prove to be correct, probably, with the insertion of one more generation. Probability, founded on the persistence of the christian name Lawrence, would lead every genealogist to attempt to connect the Virginia branch with the main line descended from John Washington of Warton and Margaret Kitson. But, in a pedigree, every fact must be susceptible of proof, and Col. Chester is entitled to the highest praise for his successful attempt to prove that the Virginia emigrants were *not* Sir John and Rev. Lawrence, the sons of Lawrence of Sulgrave and Brington, even if it now be shown that they were grandsons.

It is satisfactory, however, to have the pedigree confirmed with this small but vital correction, as it retains the value of all investigations which have been made respecting the Washingtons of Sulgrave, and will continue the interest of all Americans in what had been accepted as the birth-place of the race. Mr. Waters has interposed one more ancestor in the person of the Rev. Lawrence Washington, and we shall doubtless soon learn much more about him.

As Col. Chester's paper of 1866 may not be accessible to all of our readers, we reprint such parts as refer to Rev. Lawrence of Purleigh, especially as Mr. Waters has not cited all of them.

Extract from Col. Chester's "Preliminary Investigation."

"We proceed now to the history of LAWRENCE WASHINGTON, apparently the fifth son of Lawrence and Margaret, and certainly the younger brother of Sir William and Sir John Washington.

Baker was quite correct in stating that he was a student at Oxford in the year 1622. He was of Brasenose College, and matriculated on the 2d of November, 1621. The exact record in the Matriculation Register is as follows: 'Laurent: Washington, Northamp: Gen. fil. an. nat. 19;' *i. e.* Lawrence Washington, of Northamptonshire, whose father's rank was that of a gentleman, and whose own age was nineteen years at his last birthday.

It was not until little more than a year later that the officials commenced entering in the register the christian names and particular residences of the fathers of the students, but in the present instance the above record is almost as satisfactory as it would have been if the other particulars had been given. In the first place, the Washington family of Sulgrave, or Brington, was the only one of the name in Northamptonshire whose sons could be recognized and designated as the sons of gentlemen, unless, indeed, the Heralds of that time omitted others, which is not probable. Secondly, there was no other Lawrence Washington at Oxford for considerable periods before and after this date; unless, again, all the officials were guilty of omissions in all the Registers (for the writer has carefully examined them all), which is even more improbable. And, finally, the will of his aunt Elizabeth, widow of his uncle Robert Washington, dated on the 17th of March, 1622–3, among other legacies to his brothers and sisters, leaves him her husband's seal ring, and states that he was then at Oxford.

Lawrence Washington was born, therefore, about the year 1602. He appears to have entered at Brasenose College as early as 1619, but he did not sign the Subscription Book until the 2d of November, 1621, under which date his name also appears in the general matriculation register, in connection with thirty-five others—an extraordinary number, and indicating that from some cause this ceremony had hitherto been neglected. He took his B.A. degree in 1623, and became Fellow of Brasenose about 1624. He is recorded as serving the office of lector, then the principal educational office in the college, from 1627 to 1632 inclusive. On the 20th of August, 1631, he became one of the proctors of the university, filling a vacancy that had occurred by the deprivation of his predecessor by royal warrant. On the 14th of March, 1632–3, he was presented to the then very valuable living of Purleigh, in Essex, and resigned his fellowship. The records of a suit in Chancery, preserved at the Rolls Office, perfectly identify the rector of Purleigh with the fellow of Brasenose and the proctor of the university. He continued at Purleigh until the year 1643, when, according to Newcourt, he was 'ejected by sequestration for his loyalty in the late rebellion of 1642,' and had the honor of being pilloried in the infamous 'Century.' Walker states that he 'was afterwards permitted to have and continue upon a Living in these parts; but it was such a poor and miserable one that it was with difficulty that any one was persuaded to accept it.' The writer has been unable to ascertain the living mentioned; but it is to be hoped that some further trace of him may yet be discovered in the neighborhood of Purleigh, where, putting the usual construction upon Walker's language,* he continued in his profession of a clergyman after the Restoration, and consequently some years after the date of his namesake's emigration to Virginia."

Lastly, this important publication about the Washingtons would be imperfect if no notice were taken of the costly and widely-circulated book, published in 1879, by the late Albert Welles. Many persons have been and will be misled by this utterly false and absurd publication. I will therefore reprint the essential portions of my letter to the New York *Nation* of July 18, 1889.

The English portion was a most ridiculous performance in every point of view, and it is only fair to suppose that Mr. Welles was not in a sound state of mind when he adopted and published this statement. His unnamed English correspondent claimed to have derived his alleged facts from the Common Pleas Rolls, and adds: "The pedigree I now send I can establish by legal evidence."

* See foot-note on page 21, *ante.*—W. H. W.

The object of this pedigree was to show that several generations of Washingtons had been born at Warton, County Lancaster; that a Lawrence W. was born there in 1569, whose eldest son was Leonard W., born about 1595, the father of four sons and one daughter *baptized at Warton* in 1616, 1619, 1622, 1625, and 1627. The two younger sons were said to be Lawrence, baptized 1625, and John, baptized 1627, who were termed the emigrants to Virginia.

I will not waste time in refuting the innumerable blunders of the rest of the pedigree, but deal with the essential point here raised. Col. Chester printed a letter in the New York *World* of March 29, 1879, when he had seen the prospectus of Welles's book. He said:

"I at once recognized an old acquaintance, hawked about London some years ago, the original manuscript of which is in my own possession, and now lies on my table before me, where I keep it for the amusement of my friends. . . . I will simply select the crucial point of it, where it is stated that the two emigrant brothers, Lawrence and John Washington, were sons of Leonard Washington of Warton, and that they were respectively born and baptized in 1625 and 1627. The only possible source from which these two baptisms could be obtained is the parish register of Warton. I have examined the register personally and very carefully, and can declare that no such entries are to be found in it."

At this point I wish to introduce the evidence of the Rev. T. H. Pain, M.A., Vicar of Warton, given in a letter now before me, addressed to the *New England Historical and Genealogical Register*, dated January 25, 1889. He writes:

"I beg to say that I have not been able to find any entry of the baptism of Leonard Washington, said to have been born in Warton about 1595. As to the baptisms of his children, I send the following extracts:

Baptismata Anno Dom. 1616.
Robertus, filius Leonardi Washington, baptiz. octavo die Septembris.
Baptismat. 1619.
Jane, daughter of Leonard Washington, bapd. 4th day of September.
Bapt. Anno Dom. 1622.
Francis, ye sonne of Leonard Washington of Warton, baptized ye 4th day of February.

"*I have not been able to find an entry of the baptism of Lawrence, said to have been baptised at Warton in 1625, or of John, said to have been baptized here in 1627.*"

In the light of these two statements, no one can doubt that the pedigree is a rank and stupid forgery, made by the simple method of fastening upon Leonard Washington two sons of whom he had no knowledge, and without a word of proof.

It seems to me that Col. Chester's statement of the genesis of this forgery may be amusing and instructive. He wrote under date of June 16, 1879:

"If you could see the original, which strangely fell in my hands, you would see how the whole thing was concocted. It was got up some years ago by this 'James Phillippe' for John Camden Hotten, who died before publishing it, and his successors had too much good sense to carry out his intentions. It is evident that the compiler, after working out an elaborate pedigree, much of which I know to be false, looked about for a safe place where to put the two emigrant brothers. He finally decided to make them sons of Leonard Washington of Warton. Afterwards, probably thinking that he might be detected, he crossed out this affiliation. But, finding no better place for them, he finally wrote (as an instruction to the printer), 'This is correct.'

"Of course you would not find any proofs of his statements. This distinguished 'genealogist' never furnishes any. If asked for his authority in any instance, he draws himself up to his full height (6 ft. 4) and says, '*I* am the authority'; and that is all any one can ever get out of him. . . .

"The 'Common Pleas Rolls' are as well known to every historical student and genealogist as the Heralds' Visitations. Like all similar records, they are more or less valuable, but they rank no higher, if so high, as the 'Chancery Proceedings.' Unfortunately, they are very difficult to search, from being entirely unindexed, and it is this fact of which 'Phillippe' takes advantage. He may almost with impunity say that his authority for a particular statement is a Common Pleas roll, for unless he also gave you, which he never does, the precise year, term of court, number of roll, and number of membrane, it would be almost impossible to test his statement. I spent weeks over these rolls of the period. To say that they are not used by other genealogists is as ridiculous as to say that other genealogists do not look at wills or parish registers or any other common source of information."

Col. Chester proceeds to point out numerous specific errors, and adds:

"I have all the Washington entries of all the Registers in all the places named in the pedigree, and can say without hesitation that they can never have been consulted by the compiler. The whole affair is a mere catchpenny concern, and I am amazed at the impudence of men who can put forth such a concoction and then claim that every statement can be substantiated by legal evidence."

This indignant exposure of the fraud, from the most competent authority, will be sufficient. Every one will regret that Col. Chester did not have the good fortune to bring to a successful conclusion the investigation which he pursued for so many years. But every one will equally rejoice that the work has been accomplished by an American, and will recognize the fact that Mr. Waters has entirely filled the high place which Col. Chester left vacant.—W. H. WHITMORE.]

The following items received since the article was printed in the REGISTER are inserted in this pamphlet (see *ante*, pp. 17, 43):

Nathaniel Pope, Book No. 3, p. 279, 1000 acres on the south side of Potomac river in Westmoreland Co., Sept. 6, 1654.
William Pope, Book No. 4, p. 81, 200 acres in Westmoreland Co., March 11, 1655. [These grantees were probably brothers.]
Nathaniel Pope, Book No. 4, p. 51, 1550 acres in Westmoreland Co., April 24, 1656.
Thomas, heir to Nathaniel Pope, Book No. 4, p. 51, 1550 acres in Westmoreland Co., April 24, 1656. [the same land.]
Nathaniel Pope, Book No. 4, p. 63, 1050 acres in Westmoreland Co., Nov. 30, 1656.
Nathaniel Pope, Jr., by will, Book No. 4, p. 63, 1050 acres in Westmoreland Co., Nov. 30, 1656. [the same land.]
Lieut. Col. Nathaniel Pope, Book No. 4, p. 293, 1500 acres in Westmoreland Co., Aug. 31, 1657.
James Pope, Book No. 4, p. 376, 512 acres in Northumberland Co., Sept. 24, 1659.
James Pope, Book No. 4, p. 376, 700 acres in Northumberland Co., Sept. 24, 1659.
William Pope, Book No. 4, p. 406, 200 acres in Nansemond Co., Oct. 30, 1662.
James Pope, Book No. 4, p. 562, 700 acres in Northumberland Co., Feb. 28, 1662.
James Pope, Book No. 4, p. 563, 1000 acres in Northumberland Co., Jan. 28, 1662.
Thomas Pope, Book No. 4, p. 42, 2054 acres in Westmoreland Co., March 23, 1664.
Thomas Pope and Major John Washington, Book No. 4, p. 49, 50 acres in a parcel of islands, number ten, in Westmoreland Co., in the mouth of Cedar Creek, Sept. 4, 1661.

The above abstract of the grants to the name Pope, in our State Land Registry, is transcribed from my Memorandum book.—R. A. BROCK.

A letter has been received from Mr. Waters, dated the 20th of September, in which he states that he had visited Middle Claydon the day previous. He found there a few Roads and Verney items. The most important was the marriage, 4 April, 1668, of John Freeman and Esther Roads of Luton, in the Co. of Bedford. "Esther Roads," he writes, "was of course the daughter of William Roads, and went to her old homestead to be married. John Freeman was the one nominated by Mrs. Elizabeth Fitzherbert as one of her executors and trustees, and we now see the reason. He was her nephew by marriage. And it strengthens *much* the one weak link in our pedigree—the Tring and Luton connection.

"William Roads of Finemore was buried 28 Sept., 1657. This must have been the father of Esther Freeman, and brother of Amphillis Washington."

Mr. Waters suggests that as Fine Moor Hill, about 2½ miles south of Middle Claydon, is near a road connecting the villages of Edgecote and Quainton, the records of those places should be examined.

Amphillis, the christian name of Mrs. Washington, must be very unusual. In the Visitation of Warwickshire it occurs four times, and once in that of Leicestershire. Three of these instances are connected with the Nevill family, and it seems to be persistent in that family.—W. H. WHITMORE.

www.ingramcontent.com/pod-product-compliance
Lightning Source LLC
Chambersburg PA
CBHW021813220426
43662CB00006B/304